ULTIMATE COACHING

Skills for Developing A Highly Engaged Workforce

Chris Cebollero

ULTIMATE COACHING

Skills for Developing A Highly Engaged Workforce

By Chris Cebollero

Copyright © 2021
All Rights Reserved
ISBN: 9798589714951

Dedication

To my brother, Jay, and my nephew, Billy Meyer.
They were with me from the beginning and
will remain until the end.

Acknowledgment

There have been people in my life and career who have inspired and motivated me to become the very best person I could be, both professionally and personally. Their lessons on leadership and coaching others have been countless. These are the role models and mentors that took the time to invest in my growth by adding the values of their expertise, friendship, and love. You have my gratitude.

- Jennifer Cordia
- Ernie Rodriguez
- Ray Barishansky
- Rob Lawrence

Preface

One of the questions that I get asked usually revolves around the topic of coaching. Either it is about developing a coaching business, or the skills needed to cultivate a highly engaged workforce. When setting out to work on my next book, it seemed best to first focus on developing your foundational coaching skills.

When it comes to developing the workforce, as leaders, we do not invest in the people, those who are the backbone to organizational success and our individual success as leaders. Developing a successful workforce takes time, dedication, and honesty, a certain amount of love. Yep, I said it, love! Not only do you have to love the people you are guiding; you also have to love the responsibility of leading and coaching them. Besides an emotional connection to coaching, you must also have the skills needed to make their success happen.

This book is written by outlining the skills needed to grow the foundation you will need to develop into a great coach. The lessons cover different philosophies and foundational principles that you will need to have to ensure you are on the best path to guide someone in their life and career. For example, the first chapter covers the components of Servant Leadership. It is vital for you as the coach to be successful so that your methods are steeped in the foundation of service.

As I sat back and thought of the skills you would need to be successful, it was paramount that I stayed focused on the skills I teach others regularly. Let me give you the best coaching on how to use this book. Read the chapters, and in a separate journal, outline the following:

- What were the high points of the chapter you just read?
- Reflect on what the topic meant to you and where your skill stands today.
- Outline how you need to polish your current skill to grow those skills to the next level.
- Set goals on how you will implement these teachings.
- Finally, determine who you will focus on assisting in getting them to their next level of success.

Thank you so much for allowing me to join you on your professional development journey. Onward and upward to the next level of your success!

Cheers,
Chris Cebollero

Contents

Dedication iii
Acknowledgment iv
Preface v

Chapter 1: To Lead, You Have to Serve 1
Chapter 2: Coach Yourself First 15
Chapter 3: Feedback – It Can Be Constructive or Corrective ... 31
Chapter 4: Coaching vs. Progressive Discipline 51
Chapter 5: Motivate and Inspire the Workforce 63
Chapter 6: The Practice of Coaching 77
Chapter 7: Analyze First to Coach Best 83
Chapter 8: Coaching Low Self Confidence and
              Low Self Esteem 91
Chapter 9: Coaching High Performing Employees 99
Chapter 10: Transitioning Coaching to Mentorship 109

Conclusion 117
About the Author 119
Bibliography 123

CHAPTER 1

TO LEAD, YOU HAVE TO SERVE

The world desperately needs good leaders today. If you are running an organization, department, or project in some capacity, your employees are certainly look up to you for guidance. To help them in the best way possible, you must know and understand the art and science of leadership. I know it is easier said than done! Leadership is an immense subject that is continuously evolving, and that progression speeds up as the demands of the employee's changes. Your responsibility is to become a student of and practice the art of leadership in order to stay on top of this evolution. As a foundational leadership method, your ability to become successful leans on your ability to serve others.

To some degree or another, every individual inside your organization dreams of their ultimate success. This vision fails as those individuals do not take the necessary steps required to reach that success. This is where practicing coaching and having a footing of 'Servant Leadership' comes into play.

Your employees are the only resources inside your organization that will increase in value, and they should be developed to achieve their best results. When you have strong, happy employees, you have a strong, healthy business. Research proves that emotionally and psychologically satisfied employees work harder, are more loyal, and develop a stronger bond with the organization. Keeping in mind this knowledge, it is crucial we set off our leadership style mastering the art of servant leadership.

Understanding Servant Leadership!

*"Organizations exist to serve. Period. Leaders live to serve. Period."-**Tom Peters***

The modern workplace has changed, and there is no place for a "boss" in it. On the other hand, when you talk about the accomplishment of successful leaders, every company would welcome them with open arms. Before we dive into the components of servant leadership, I want to just take a moment to outline the difference between a leader and a boss. Leadership is all about action; they take on the responsibility of leading people. Bosses or managers manage things, processes, procedures. You lead people, and you manage things. This is where you must differentiate yourself, as you actively take the journey to become a successful, influential leader.

It is important to understand the role and responsibilities you have and what is required for you to become a successful leader. What makes an ideal leader? Someone with the employees' best interest at heart, one that helps members of the workforce achieve greatness, motivates them, inspires them, polishes their skills, and helps them realize their goals.

A leader's main goal is to focus on coaching, growing, listening, and understanding members of the workforce. In doing so, you will create a diverse community and lead it by example. If you are reading this book, it is safe to presume that you seek to understand the science behind becoming the best coach and leader possible.

There are many different types of leadership styles, and as a good leader, you must use a smattering of styles to be successful.

Still, the foundation of any great leader has to be focused on the components of service and being a servant leadership.

Servant leadership is a philosophy, a timeless concept that has changed the world. Even though Robert K. Greenleaf coined the term in the late 1970s, its ideology has existed for centuries. It is nothing new, but only now has the business world started paying attention to the magnitude practicing this style holds.

It is a philosophy that gives attention to the enrichment of individuals and creates an organization that strives for excellence and success. Being a servant leader is a big responsibility; this is where one selflessly focuses on the needs of others instead of their own. It's not something people instinctively do. People do not work for you. Instead, you actually work for them, and it is paramount that you try your best to understand their needs.

Countless people confuse servant leadership as just another style of leadership. Please do not make that mistake because, in the end, it is not merely a technique or a method. It is more of an attitude and a way to achieve ultimate leadership success. With servitude, you naturally acknowledge people and their perspectives. You make them part of your decisions; they feel safe and trust working with you.

They also believe they are a part of your organization, take ownership of the vision, and know their importance in achieving that vision. Consequently, people will also be motivated to improve their knowledge, skills, and traits under a good servant leadership environment.

Think about it as a leader, don't you want to be the kind of person your employees trust, love, and look up to? I know it sounds like a weird question, but as a leader, when your employees love working for you, they will be loyal, and more importantly, they will follow you.

Suppose we observe it from a business point of view. In that case, it is natural that empowered employees perform at a much higher level, bringing innovative ideas forward, becoming engaged, and focus their efforts on supporting the success of the company. These employees now become driven toward success and are more involved in achieving organizational goals. When you are able to motivate them, empower them, and show them a future, watch what happens!

Organizations that practice servant leadership will tell you that it increases their employee retention, have low turnover, and a highly engaged workforce that is productive. When the workforce works in an environment that fosters a community of servant leadership, it opens doors for adaptability, creativity, and development.

Remember, no one can stop the impending change that is about to hit the business world, but when you have an adaptive workforce, that change is seamless.

There is a dramatic shift in today's work environment, where disruption and uncertainty are becoming the norm. Such a rapid change in the work environment demands adaptability and modernization of workflows and processes. Examine your workforce and determine if your employees are ready for such a change. If not, then it is your responsibility to lead them in the right direction. Thus, employees must be more energetic, bring more innovation to the table, and show more commitment toward their organizations. However, finding such employees can certainly be a challenge. That is why it is so important to grow the workforce that can take you into the next decade of business. This is the premise for coaching and making your workforce into the best force possible. Teaching and guiding them toward such a mentality require a straightforward process that can easily be implemented.

Ten Components of Servant Leadership

Greenleaf tried his best to show the world the importance of servant leadership. So, when Greenleaf was coming up with its concept, he had to think of the most suitable analogy. For that, he chose 'The Journey to the East by Hermann Hesse,' a book that tells the story of a group exploring new nations and lands.

Among the group members is a servant, Leo. He sings for them, dances for them, and takes care of their stuff. One day Leo disappears, and his loss is significantly felt by the group. As all the group members without Leo disperse, break up, and end up going on their separate paths, you realize how crucial he was for the group's success.

In the end, we find that Leo was the natural leader of the group all along. Inspired by this, Greenleaf realized that achieving authentic leadership is only possible through serving. He highlighted ten characteristics that explain servant leadership based on this example.

Listening – The first component and maybe the most important one is listening and really active listening. It often becomes hard for bosses to pay attention to their employees. They rarely take-out time to listen to them. In return, employees end up feeling less important and alienated. So, you must actively listen to your employees as a servant leader, and you should also take advice from those employees that are doing their job with dedication and commitment. No one knows the job better than those doing the work.

Their success is the true measurement of your success. There is a big difference between just listening and active listening. With active listening, you not only hear your employee's words, but you feel the emotions hidden in them. I have been saying for years, stop listening to their words and instead start paying attention to their feelings.

You must pay attention to the hidden details of their message, make good eye contact, and make them feel that they are the most crucial component of the conversation, and watch your influence grow. Remember, their advice, needs, and ideas can often benefit the business, save costs, and boost employee morale. In the end, this is a small price to pay for an outstanding return on investment. In summary, make sure that you actively listen to your employees.

Empathy – The second component that helps you connect on a deeper level with your employees is empathy. Striving to understand your employees is vital but is often a missing element of the professional relationship. When you fail to see them as people with emotional needs, they will most certainly feel distant. You can teach people what to do, but you can never teach them how to feel; this is why you need to understand their feelings and teach them how to let their feelings positively guide them.

I have had people come into my office, sharing troubles with their schedule, pay, partners, and coworkers. Believe it or not, I had the same problems when I used to work in the field, as well. So, I understand their point of view. Because I can certainly relate with my employees, it gives me an empathetic perspective on their issues. Don't just listen to their problems but help by creating constructive solutions with them.

Sometimes, a kind heart is all it takes to be a successful leader.

Healing – The third component is healing. Our people are emotional beings with emotional needs, and sometimes those feelings can get hurt. Healing can be a powerful tool that brings workforce transformation. For example, somebody didn't get a promotion, or maybe there is the perception the manager doesn't like them, this could eventually lead to creating a toxic or negative attitude. Such situations deviate employees from their path, and it is your responsibility to bring them back to the fold. It is vital that everyone feels like they are part of the organization's vision and mission. This is where the healing begins. Regardless of what has happened in the past, it is the leader's responsibility to show the workforce they are part of the organization, and you profoundly care about them. You should try to heal them.

Self-Awareness – The fourth component requires a little bit of self-study and insight; it is self-awareness. We, as humans, are imperfect and prone to making mistakes based on emotions. Acceptance will allow you to reflect on your emotions and why you react the way you do and develop the knowledge to strengthen your self-awareness skills.

Therefore, we should ask ourselves who we are as leaders and individuals. We need to know our strengths and weaknesses. Once we have a better knowledge of our shortcomings, we can work hard to improve them. This will make us more self-aware. We also need to understand how we react to a situation and, more importantly, why we react to a situation. No matter what we do in life, we can never reach the pinnacle of ultimate success if we don't understand ourselves.

Persuasion – The fifth component is the art of persuasion, and it is vital to lead others. As leaders, people must be willing to follow us to the depths of the ocean. We must get them on board in the direction the organization is heading. In the old days, the approach was just to tell them this is the way it's going to be.

This is kind of the "my way or the highway" approach to running an organization. It's is an important concept to understand, but more importantly, the days of command and control and leading from a position of authority are over. As we move forward, introducing new processes, we must persuade people around us that this is the way to go.

The best way to implement positive changes happens when you persuade your workforce that this is the way to go. Suppose you include your employees in decision-making from the beginning and let them see the 'why'. They will understand the change better and cope with it accordingly. Servant leaders must seek and build consensus by letting other people see the how and why they may not have yet considered. Change can be an uncomfortable concept in an organization. Give people a chance to talk about their feelings throughout the process, and then ask how you can make it easier for them to adapt to the change.

Conceptualization – The sixth component, teaching you how to dream big, is conceptualization. You must be able to cast a big vision for organizational success. You should see the vision in your mind and mentally draw it out like a picture.

You need to share that organizational vision and let everyone know what their responsibility is in reaching that vision. Consequently, this is what leads to developing success with your employees. As humans, we are wired to think in pictures. If I ask you to think about a door, you will not see the letters 'DOOR.' Instead, you will create its mental image. Hence, people must understand what excellence and success will look like once they get there.

Then they need to know their responsibilities in helping the organization achieve its vision. As key stakeholders, we must share our vision with them and watch them reach that big vision.

Foresight – The seventh component, which can be hard at times, is foresight. A good servant leader is wise. Thus, predicting the future with the experience of hindsight of your past becomes vital. Think about the past, especially consider your mistakes, lessons learned, and successes. Make sure that you don't make the same ones again. An excellent equation to remember is *Mistakes + Reflection = Wisdom*. We must lead our workforce with foresight. If an employee is choosing the wrong path, you can tell them, "*I tried that once before, and it didn't work out for me. But go ahead and give it a shot.*" Doing this will allow the employee to learn from both your experience and theirs. Such is the nature of foresight that sharing your mistakes with your employees can help them avoid doing the same and assist them with a significant learning experience.

Stewardship – The eighth component, which relies heavily on trust, is stewardship. It is the ethics that embodies responsible planning for resource management. You have a responsibility to ensure that you grow people, not waste money, and develop the best products possible. You must ensure that you direct the organization to a better position tomorrow than you found it yesterday. Stewardship means that you build trust and confidence among your employees. You must give your best as it is your responsibility, and your employees must feel the same way. Even if their values differ from the organization, they are obliged to give their best.

Commitment to Growing People – The ninth component, which is a reflection on the kind of leader you are, is the commitment to your people's growth. Helping your employees grow is the foundation of coaching. People go through vigorous steps to join our organizations. Once they join us, they help us achieve our goals and bring success to the company. Knowing this, we should treat them with the respect they deserve. We, as leaders, need to get the best out of them by empowering them.

Let's assume that a new member of the workforce joins your organization and has the knowledge level of a 5 on the 10-scale in a specific task. We must now ask ourselves; do we want them to stay at a 5 or assist in developing them to a 10? If we focus on their development, we enhance our production and maximize efforts. In this situation, don't only think about your company but also pay attention to the good deed of developing human resources.

By helping your employees, you are teaching them to be better at what they do. You will find them grateful to you for the rest of their lives. So, you must commit to people's growth to move your organization to the next level. When we grow our workforce, we grow our organization. We need to decide the best way to develop each individual, which we can achieve by active listening. Ask them where they see themselves in the next couple of years, or what their goals are, or find out what they want to get out of their positions, try to identify their weakness, and strengths. Once you gather this information develop a personal improvement plan that takes them to the next level.

Building Community – The tenth and the last component is building a community. People who are a part of a larger group, working together toward a single goal, will always be stronger than individuals. Having a group mentality means that your workforce will support each other and offer help to realize mutual goals.

Also, diversity is the future of globalization. We have different beliefs, religions, morals, values, political opinions, and goals. Still, people with such differences work in the same organization, the same department, and the same team. People must realize this remarkable fact. Even if you possess a different mindset than your coworker, you have to understand that no one tells you to invite them to your home, cook a meal for them, or share a drink with them. Yet, you still need to respect them as equal individuals. We should not demean them with jokes, judge them, or make them feel uncomfortable. Instead, we must create a welcoming environment where everybody feels a part of a larger family. Sexism, racism, and differences have no place in the modern workplace. We should rise above such old-fashioned mentalities and learn to work well by leveraging our diversity.

Drawbacks of Command-and-Control Management

People who work in your chain of responsibility must never take assigned tasks as a command. Instead, they should be on board with you, understanding your vision, and following you with their heart. To achieve this, we have to let go of the traditional 'Command and Control' style of management.

Alternatively, you must focus on a more facilitative and collaborative culture. That is something you achieve through transparency and honesty, and this will make your employees trust the organization more and help them achieve organizational goals. Employees can also feel motivated when their leadership supports them in all work-related tasks.

Now, the biggest problem with the Command and Control' style of management is that managers fail to create a relationship with their employees. Employees look at their managers as machines that never cease to nag and even think that they are inhumane and void of emotions at times. When managers turn to an authoritative or commanding approach, they often tend to degrade, demotivate, and devalue their employees. Employees have a decreased desire to contribute to their firms when facing such challenges. They become less productive in general, and this ends up costing companies a lot. This is the total opposite of what we are trying to achieve by coaching our workforce to excellence.

So, initiating a sense of responsibility and motivating them to work from their heart is the ultimate secret of success. Command and Control management can only motivate employees extrinsically, such as offering monetary benefits, threatening employees, and showing authority. At the same time, we as servant leaders must pay attention to their intrinsic needs. Giving them a sense of ownership makes them feel good about the work they do psychologically. Involving them in company decisions, giving them proper tools, and making them feel essential will produce more positive results. As a leader, you must understand that people should like you and agree with you. People will naturally work harder for a person they like, appreciate, and respect. Creating such values is vital for success. Not only that, but employees can feel like a family working toward the same goals, especially if they agree with your direction. Do you want subjects to rule over, or would you prefer people who genuinely follow you? Help your employees and coach them in the best way possible. This is why we need to explore what 'coaching' means.

Coaching your Employees

If you plan on being a leader, be prepared to teach, guide, and help. This is the whole foundation of Servant Leadership. Employees often require proper guidance and turn to their leaders for it, bringing us to the importance of coaching. It is the cornerstone of servant leadership, and you must engrave it into our everyday responsibility. Coaching is not merely helping or guiding employees into building their personal and professional skills, but it teaches them self-worth, grows self-confidence, and develops the next generation leader.

As we get ready to close out this chapter when practicing coaching and create a 'true learning' environment and where the process of learning never ceases, you cultivate the foundation of individual and hence organizational success. With the practice of Servant Leadership and using all its components, you are creating an environment that will allow your workforce to feel that you are the leader that they want to follow. Once you get them engaged, satisfied, and productive, you can grow their skills, knowledge, and experience that will, without a doubt, grow your organization.

Coaching is not limited to sharing your knowledge and skills with employees. It is about recognizing one's potential and unlocking it to the maximum level. There will be those who might fail to realize their potential, and that is where you need to help them see it. A great leader and coach will need to see the potential in others before they see it in themselves. As we continue ahead, we will further explore the prospects of coaching in detail and why it is an essential tool to become a successful servant leader.

CHAPTER 2

COACH YOURSELF FIRST

When we think about coaching and motivating the members of a workforce, we know it is essential for any leader. Remember, as we begin this chapter, leadership is an action, a verb, not a noun. It is not in a title, achievement, or position. It is all in your actions through which you can influence people to follow you. If you can influence them, you can or are already leading them.

Yet, one of the missing components to being successful at motivating others is the failure to keep ourselves motivated. In fact, this is the part we often neglect. Self-leadership and self-motivation are the toughest tasks you will have to master in your professional career. To be honest, motivation is one of the most significant missing attributes of many leaders out there.

This is why this chapter focuses solely on self-motivation and being your own coach first before you can coach someone else.

Why do we fail when it comes to Self-Motivation?

Before I get into self-motivation, I want to share a bit about the missing component that leads to failure in this department. A secret here is, what if I tell you this isn't necessarily an issue of the lack of self-motivation?

Let's create a scenario to better understand what I am trying to say. It is New Year's Eve! There is excitement in the atmosphere for the New Year. As we enjoy our umpteenth adult beverage, telling our big fish stories, we always get around to the inevitable New Year's Resolution. *"This year, I am going to get into better shape." "This year, I am going to find a new job." "This year, I am going to get married." "This year, I am going to graduate."* Then as the New Year goes on, we forget about the goals we had set in the beginning, and we are right back on the same page we were on the previous New Year's Eve, a page with a list of things we wanted and wished to do. So, what really happened? Why are we stuck on the first page? Let's look at this in a different way.

We set a goal with good intentions to turn it into a reality. However, there are always some speed bumps, hurdles, and obstacles along the journey that seem to get in the way. That's when we get derailed from the initial goal, and the chances are, we may even forget about them.

Now, there is a secret behind this failure. One of the primary reasons we fail is not because of the lack of motivation or commitment to a goal but because we have not developed the 'habit' of adding this new goal of 'what we want' to our already established daily routine.

Think about it. Let's assume you wish to lose weight. Ask yourselves, where does losing weight fit into your daily routine, or are you planning on going to the gym? The missing component in reaching your goal of success is where it will fit into your everyday schedule?

When we set off to develop a new goal, we must remember to make space for this goal and find out where it fits into our daily routine. Les Brown has a great quote that helps us understand how we need to adjust ourselves according to our goal:

"To get something you've never gotten, you have to do something you have never done."

You must be prepared to give up on something to get something. If you are looking for the next big success or achieving a new goal in the same everyday habits, you will never find it. If it were there, you would have already found it. You will have to create a new daily routine for something new you want to add to your ambitions. You must be ready to give something up to adjust something new—more on that in a minute.

You have to break the chain of your already established daily routine or maybe replace something old with something new. People ask me all the time, *"How the heck are you finding the time to write some of the greatest and most outstanding leadership books around?"* To be honest, they are only asking: How do I find the time to write books? I threw the "greatest and "most outstanding" in just for dramatic effect. When you're an author, you get to add a dramatic flair every now and again.

All the fun aside, I found the time to write by giving something up and creating a new daily routine. As I began this project, I spent an hour every evening watching Seinfeld, which makes around five hours a week watching mindless TV. However, when I started putting my pen down on the paper for this work, I gave up my one hour of TV time and dedicated it to solely writing every night.

The Habit Loop

Yes, there is something called the habit loop that we take into account when we wish to develop new habits. The loop has three components: the trigger, the routine, and the reward.
1. **The Trigger** – This is also known as the cue. This is what triggers the habit to occur. They usually fall under the categories of location, time of the day, seeing other people, and emotional

state of mind. When a trigger takes place, it causes the behavior. For instance, a part of my daily routine is waking up at 5 AM and going to the gym. The cue is my alarm going off, and it is time to get out of bed.

2. **The Routine** – This helps begin the process of the behavior you want to change. Once you have the goal, let's say I want to go to the gym, the trigger woke me up, and the routine is now getting out of bed and starting my car with the auto start. This now gives me 15 minutes to get myself washed, teeth brushed, dressed, and out the door.

3. **The Reward** – This is where the brain steps in and starts to see the results, reinforcing the routine. When you begin to see the desired behavior of wanting to go to the gym, you are more likely to continue the practice. So, now it's the habit that you've created, which makes self-motivation easier.

What is Self-Motivation?

The definition of self-motivation is – *Being able to find the ability to do what needs to be done without any influence from other people or situations.* It is where we turn the 'shoulds' into 'musts.'

This is really about boosting and encouraging yourself to make continuous positive progress toward your goal. Sometimes, there are hurdles, challenges, and speedbumps as I mentioned above. But the trick is when those unexpected things pop up, to allow the momentum you built to continue the roll of your journey. I will say this a couple times in this book, it is not reaching the goal that gives you the growth. Reaching the goal is just the extra gravy. It is the journey you take in reaching the goal where the growth comes. It is what you learn, what mistakes you make, any failures you have to overcome. That's where the growth comes from.

Let's be honest here; life is not without challenges. Those challenges love to pop up when things are going well, and we are getting to the point of putting everything on cruise control. When you feel as though your journey will hit a huge rock, instead of getting derailed, know that this is just part of your journey's growth and use your critical thinking skills to choose the best way to right the ship. In simpler words, you must stay on the right path toward achieving your goal, regardless of what happens. This is where the secret sauce of desire comes into play. More on the importance of desire in a moment.

An example is the great COVID-19 pandemic we are all facing today. When 2020 started, I had set some great goals for myself, including writing this book, creating a 10-week course on developing your self-mastery. I also had 90 live motivational talks scheduled. As part of my New Year goals, I had also set an amount of money I want to make during that year. Then the COVID-19 pandemic arrived and was a huge speedbump that affected not only my journey but everyone else's. All of us went through dealing with the pandemic hurdles. We are in a lockdown, practicing social distancing, and numerous businesses have been closed down since practically the beginning of the year. I lost about 60% of my speaking engagements, rescheduled live mastermind classes and workshops, and lost approximately 70% of my client base (hang on, I need a shot of tequila).

The speed bumps and barriers that became a hurdle between my 2020 goals' success are enough to make anyone drink excessively. However, how did I handle this major decline in my business? I stayed true to my goals, and I knew losing my client base and speaking engagements would not allow me to make the money I set as a goal for 2020. Still, on a brighter side, here is the book I always wanted to write on coaching, and the courses I wanted to create are completed on time and ready for presentation. Remember this, as I mentioned earlier, life does not exist entirely without speedbumps and hurdles, but reaching the goal is not where your growth stems it's the journey. 2020, the year of COVID-19 sucks, but I decided to stay true to my vision of success in reaching my goals and staying as positive as possible. When you are on your journey, you must stay true to your path and make your goals come true.

Desire – The fuel of your success

One of the first lessons I learned while in the military was how to make fire. During Land Survival training, the instructors went through the science of making fire. You need to have three things to create fire: fuel, spark, and oxygen.

Let's discuss these elements in the current scenario. Your goal is the spark, self-motivation is the oxygen, and desire is the fuel. If your fuel is wet, it won't catch fire, and as a result, your fire will fail. If your desire is not burning hot and deep enough to start a fire, your goal will fail.

In the book 'Think and Grow Rich,' Napoleon Hill tells us that *"desire is the starting point of all achievements."* It seems that wishing often takes the place of a good burning desire. We have all wished for something. *I wish I could write a book. I wish I could find a better job. I wish I could lose weight and many more, etc.* But what does wishing for things really bring us? Nothing but more depression, frustration, and negative feelings! You must stop wishing and put a plan in place to turn that wish into a reality. This is the fuel, the burning desire that will help you make your vision, your goal, come true.

Have you ever wanted something so bad that you could actually taste it? Something you have wanted to achieve so eagerly that nothing was going to get in the way of you attaining it. Pause reading for a minute to think about what it was and remember that feeling of being unstoppable as though you could conquer the entire world.

It was the **desire** and the **will** to reach that particular goal. That vision was strong enough to steamroll over anyone if they got in your way. It made your desire for success **hot**.

On the flip side of that coin, when that desire is not at a boiling point and not burning hot enough for you to succeed, your goal will fail. When you allow yourself to become derailed, this will stop you in your tracks, and you will eventually give up. Then, you make excuses, blame others, and forget your goal's journey. When this happens, you do not have a strong enough desire, and that is when you will need to reevaluate your vision to make that desire hot again.

It happens, not because your vision or goal is wrong, but because you have not created a strong enough vision to create the fuel needed to succeed. That strong vision allows that desire to burn strongly enough to make that vision a reality.

Let's look at it from a different perspective. Who has the right to stop you from achieving that goal? Who has the right to say you can't do that or be successful at it? Who has the right to say that you can't start a business of your own? That you cannot get that degree! We all know that answer: no one has the right to get in the way of your plans, goals, and successes. Well, almost no one, because in reality, someone has the power to stop you from achieving your goals, and that someone is you. You give yourself the permission and the power to derail your vision.

As humans, you can provide yourself with the power to succeed or the power to sabotage success. I know it's a cliché, but I am going to say it anyway, *we are our worst enemy.*

That voice in our head that is there every day throwing up roadblocks, building up those hurdles, and helping put excuses in our way to stop our progress. We do it to ourselves, and what is more horrible about that statement is that we allow it to happen. Then, ladies and gentlemen, we look to blame everyone and everything else but ourselves.

We make excuses for our own shortcomings. That voice puts us in a place where we are no longer motivated. An inferiority complex takes over. It makes us feel like a failure, and we do not feel worthy of anything.

Remember this one thing, the voice in your head is coming from your own subconscious mind and is only saying what you have programmed it to say. You know what you are telling yourself, *I am never going to be wealthy, I am never going to be successful, I am a failure, a bad parent,* and perhaps, a terrible spouse.

Your subconscious mind has no ability to think or give a reason. It is only repeating back to you what you have told it to believe a thousand times.

Now, this is where a positive mindset must take over for you. It has to be in everything you do. In my book, Ultimate Success: Strategic Leadership Excellence, there is a chapter, 'You Are the Difference Maker,' which is all about having a positive attitude. So, when you are finding it challenging to keep your positive attitude because of negative thoughts, always continue to challenge them with a positive voice. Always see the positive in everything. Never allow your thoughts to submit to the negative abyss of your inner talk.

When you think positively, you attract positive energy. It is the positive attitude that makes all things possible. When I am looking for motivation, thinking things will never change, I look toward the injured Veterans coming back from the war. They are very inspiring and continue to fight, now that they are home. These heroes must learn to walk, speak and even feed themselves again. They have to learn to live a normal and healthy life after having their arms, legs, and part of their faces blown off. It's like somebody pushed a restart button in their life, and now they have to do everything from the very start. They don't give in to their circumstances. Do you know why? It's because there is a desire that burns strong in them to be something more than just a causality.

So, how can you create a burning desire on your own? Let's spend a couple of paragraphs talking about some elements that help create a strong burning desire.

How to Create A Burning Desire?

Just a piece of easy advice as you set forward on the journey of creating a burning desire: The stronger the desire you feel, the stronger the opportunity for you to be successful. So, let's work on something together right now. There has to be something you want to achieve or have wanted for some time. Think about it and bring it to the front of your mind. I want you to pick a goal. Come on, play along! You are reading this book to be inspired, to learn how to coach and inspire others. This is the basis for this whole chapter of self-leadership and self-motivation. Let's make today 'day one' instead of one day. Let's take out some time and work on your goal together. Are you ready?

Elements of Goal Setting

We can put setting and reaching your goal into six easy steps. Ladies and gentlemen, I promise you, if you follow these six steps, you will be able to make any goal that you have set for yourself strong enough to see it through till the end. This is also the method you will use with your workforce when you guide them to reach their goals. Hence, it is good to practice the technique.

The Steps

1. **Be definitive and specific about your goal** – When you are looking to set a goal, it is vital to be as precise as possible. 'I want to lose weight' is never a good goal. 'I want to lose 10 pounds' is specific.

2. **Set a new routine** – To reach your goal, you must determine precisely what you have to give in return. As the saying goes, *to get something you have never gotten, you have to do something you have never done.* So, in your daily routine, what are you giving up in reaching this goal. I've said it before, and it fits here too, if you are looking for new success with the same everyday habits, you won't find it. You must break the routine and do something new.

3. **Establish a definite date to end this journey** – A goal is a dream with a deadline. You must ask yourselves, *"What is the deadline for my dream?"* Going back to the goal of wanting to lose 10 pounds, when do you want this to happen? Then stay true to that date. If you need to add some time, that's okay. Just stay committed to completing it on that date.

4. **Create a step-by-step plan** – This fourth step is often overlooked in goal setting. You now need to develop a step-by-step plan on how you will reach this goal. Develop the strategy that will determine how you will make this goal a reality. You must establish the steps necessary to assist you in getting to the end result. What do you have to do? When do you have to begin? Who do you have to become? Outline the plan and then faithfully follow it and write it down. One of the keys to success here is that you may need to find a role model or mentor who knows how to navigate these waters. Just know that it is okay to seek that advice and help when planning for a goal.

5. **Vision Statement** – Now, these next two steps are incredibly important. It is all about the vision of reaching the goal. Develop a brief, clear statement of what you want to achieve, when you want to achieve it, and why you want to do it. What will it do for you once you achieve it? How will it make you feel? How important is it to you? Make this as positive as you can to ensure optimal motivation.

6. **Read this vision statement twice out loud every day** – When you read it, you start to believe it in your heart and mind. Even begin to think to yourself that you have already achieved this goal. This way, you are adding fuel to the fire of your desire. More importantly, you are now in the process of rewiring your subconscious mind. The two best times to read this statement are before you close your eyes to sleep and when you first wake up in the morning. The reason behind this is easy to guess. When you wake up in the morning, you plan the day ahead of you, and when you are going to bed at night, you set goals for the next day. So, it's better to remind yourself of the most vital goal for you at these moments. Your vision statement should be a part of how you plan your every day.

Creating Self-Motivation

Following all the six steps and all that we discussed earlier, we have finally gotten to the secrets for creating positive self-motivation. In 1988, artist Bobby McFerrin released a song that everybody at the time seemed to be singing or quoting, *"Don't Worry Be Happy."* This is where I developed the 'don't worry be happy' methodology of self-motivation. Okay, there is no real methodology. It only sounded pretty scientific, but I digress.

There is something to be said about practicing being happy and as positive as possible. Remember, we cannot control what happens to us or around us. However, we can, in fact, control how we react to it. Keep repeating in your mind, *don't worry be happy*, and you will see it reflect in your actions. When you focus on being positive and happy, you are less likely to become derailed and needlessly procrastinate. Now, I have that song stuck in my head, and I am going to need to get a sandwich or something and sing awhile.

The Ease of Procrastination

Procrastination is all about letting yourself off the hook for something you promised yourself you would do. You are giving yourself justification and an excuse to fail.

It's the *"yeah, but"* monster coming to visit and stay for a while. *Yeah, but I don't have the money! Yeah, but I am tired today! Yeah, but it's raining!* You know what? *Yeah, but my ass!* Stop the excuses and gift yourself the success you deserve.

Another best practice to win in this space is to take charge of all the negative feelings and negative self-talk that plague your day. No one can make you feel anything you choose not to feel. Remember that. Stay positive and remember the song, *don't worry be happy*. Heck, even the Seven Dwarfs whistled while they worked. Challenge that negative self-talk with positive affirmation, and soon, you will notice the difference. Read the vision statement you wrote for your goal again.

Focus on the goal for your success and stay productive throughout the day. There is research out there that tells us that people are more productive when they are positive and happy.

Going back to when I was in the military and back to my Land Survival Training. It was a truly interesting experience. We had the chance to learn how to live off the land and keep ourselves safe despite the environment or any challenges. Part of that school included instruction on escape and evasion, i.e., dealing with POW situations. This was a very important part of the course.

Retrospectively, you know what that school taught us. It wasn't survival, or how to escape, or make tools, or how to feed ourselves. It taught us the power of optimism; how to stay positive in the face of ultimate negativity. It was all about believing in who we were and that everything would work out for the best as long as we stayed positive. In short, it taught us all about the power of the will to survive. When you have the will to survive and are optimistic and positive, you are winning in every situation.

Tips for Self-Motivation

Now, you have your goal and are fueling your desire, which should be burning hot. This now becomes the time to get your self-motivation kicked into a higher gear, as well. Here are some steps to keep you focused on completing your goal. These are things that you do outwardly to be successful.

1. **Time Management** – On the tasks for self-motivation is that you need to learn how to manage time. This is a necessary tool when you are working toward something significant. Remember your vision. Your goal has a time limit. You have set an end date, and you must stay true to this time. This is where time management is crucial. For the record, I believe we cannot truly manage time, but instead, we manage our processes within time. A great method for managing a process, and something I have been using for over 15 years, is called 'time blocking,' but that is a concept for a whole other book. But there are tons of lessons online for you to check out.

2. **Look for role models on the subject** – I know I have said this before but, look for the success of others. Try to find someone who has done what you are trying to do and seek their counsel. Ask for their advice, have them mentor you through. We do not do this enough. We let our ego take over. However, my business as a coach is entirely based on this concept. People

want to attain what I have attained, and they seek my help to share my knowledge, to share my how, share my why, my expertise, learn from my failures, the lessons learned, and everything in between.

3. **Be grateful** – It may sound silly, but you are alive, have opportunities, and have the ability. Think about those who are less fortunate than you and what they would give to have the life you are living. So, always be grateful.

4. **Picture your vision statement** – Keep it in front and center of your mind. I can promise you, folks; visualization is the key to your Ultimate Success.

5. **Keep moving forward** – Take the baby steps toward your vision and deadline every day. You must keep the momentum rolling, and once it starts, don't allow it to stop. You deserve this gift, and you deserve to reach this goal, enjoy the journey, and learn something new from your experience every day. Remember, it is not about reaching the goal, but it is also experiencing the journey where you grow.

6. **Strengthen your body** – Walk, workout, go for a hike, or ride a bicycle, do something to help your body get stronger. We are trying to strengthen your mind here, but your body needs the same focus and attention. Pro tip: Listen to your favorite music while you are working out. It will help you stay motivated and enjoy the process.

7. **Develop strong self-awareness** – Self-awareness is one of the most essential qualities that you can have for developing your success. If you do not understand who you are as an individual, why you respond or react the way you do, there is no chance of achieving your *Ultimate Success*.

8. **Celebrate small wins** – It sounds so simple, but it is often overlooked. I have a friend who lost over 300 pounds. Of course, the question is, *"How did you lose 300 pounds?"*

I indeed asked this question. Their response was, *"I did not lose 300 pounds at once. At first, I lost 9 pounds, then 10 pounds, then 5 pounds, and then 12 pounds."* When he reached those small wins, he rewarded himself with a burger, some pizza, or an ice cream sundae, whatever reward he had set for that particular target.

These tips are the best techniques to keep you motivated enough to reach your goal and keep the burning desire alive. We have covered lots of topics in this block of instructions. However, one of the main things that I hope you take from this chapter is that if you cannot lead with confidence and self-motivate yourself, you will have a hard time convincing other to follow your guidance. Be an expert in change so others will accept your influence to change.

Do you want to be a coach? What was that goal you wrote down a few paragraphs above? Take it seriously, start working on it today, and coach yourself to that goal's completion. Then you are ready to coach others.

CHAPTER 3

FEEDBACK – IT CAN BE CONSTRUCTIVE OR CORRECTIVE

"We all need people who will give us feedback. That's how we improve." -**Bill Gates**

When was the last time you told your employee that they did a great job? Was there an occasion that you felt that they could have done a better job? Did you say anything to them? Regardless of the reason, leaders are not interacting with their workforce as much as they should in order to polish their performance. Feedback, whether constructive or corrective, is important to developing individual growth.

Do you remember anything one of your teachers said to you that kept you motivated to keep doing better? Teachers are good for this. Something that made you feel like they saw something in you, and they believe in you more than you believe in yourself. I am sure there is always that one teacher wanting to make a difference. The words they gave always gave a little spark to want to do better. This is the power of and importance of feedback in our lives.

What Is 'Feedback?'

Feedback is a term that describes helpful information or criticism from an individual about a previous behavior or action communicated to an individual or a group of individuals. When delivered correctly, people can use it to adjust and improve their current and future practices.

For instance, a customer's reaction to the company's products, services, or policies is called 'customer feedback.' This is a big part of how we learn our company is doing overall from the consumer standpoint. Similarly, 'employee performance feedback' is the employees' reaction to feedback from their manager or leader – when giving feedback, the exchange of information involves both: the expected performance and the exhibited performance.[1] This allows the best opportunity for creating success.

We are going to discuss corrective and constructive feedback in a bit. This type of feedback is always positive and never demeaning. There's no doubt that feedback is a good thing and usually always has healthy outcomes. Anyone can and needs to benefit from great feedback regularly.

A feedback-rich culture where people are comfortable receiving and asking for feedback from their colleagues and managers can actually prove beneficial for the overall business. It can truly change how the workplace operates and performs. What is important here is to note how often do we truly give out feedback? Most times, we are sharing feedback when things go bad. In many organizations, feedback is only given once a year, often during appraisals or annual reviews.

Think about it a second, can you remember the last time someone gave you any feedback on your performance at work? If it did not take just a few seconds to remember one, it's obvious that it was too long ago. Though receiving feedback can be daunting for people, it is required if you want to create teams that perform well and are motivated. Here are a few reasons why feedback is essential.

---

[1] *5 Reasons Why Feedback is Important*, Retrieved from https://www.snapsurveys.com/blog/5-reasons-feedback-important/

It Provokes Change and Fuels Growth

Feedback allows people to look at themselves in a different light. It serves as a mirror and shows how others perceive them and how they create an impact on others around them. This can be insightful, particularly for leaders, since it can help them in finding ways of creating more trust and inspiring their teams to perform better.

Most people want to succeed in their work. It is human nature, which is why people are often very receptive to constructive feedback. Most people feel that their performance would improve if their managers provided corrective feedback on a regular basis. In fact, people prefer to receive positive corrective feedback as well as praise and recognition.

It Gives People A Sense of Purpose

Who doesn't like to feel appreciated? As humans, we all like to have a sense of belonging. This means that it is essential employees feel they are important, and they bring value to what they do and to the workplace itself. As professionals, we are always trying to improve our performance when we feel that we are a part of a broader team – a whole system – all working toward the same goals. Your employees must see themselves as a brick in a wall; even if a single brick is missing, the wall cannot stand firm. Knowing that we are useful and valued gives us a sense of purpose. It makes us feel that there is some meaning to what we do. It motivates people to show up each day and give their best. Regular feedback is a way of showing people that they are valued and useful. Even negative feedback can encourage people to want to do better. Of course, that negative feedback needs to be given in the most positive of ways. Feedback, whether good or bad, can serve as a reminder to your employees that there is a point to all their work.

It Improves Employee Engagement

A study shows that 4 in 10 workers are automatically discouraged and perform lower when receiving little or no feedback. The following study also highlighted numerous reasons why employees must receive regular feedback. 43% of employees who highly engage in work receive feedback at least once a week compared to 18% of employees with low engagement. Employees crave feedback, even if they don't say it.

It Helps Improve Working Relationships

When you receive feedback from a co-worker, it opens up new communication channels between employees. It can particularly be useful if there is a conflict or tension between colleagues. Giving feedback creates an opportunity to find ways to work together better and get things out in the open to resolve hidden issues. Moreover, regular feedback can prevent conflict from happening in the first place. Before small issues have a chance to escalate into something bigger, they can be resolved with a strong culture of communication.

Employees must receive feedback about how they perform and how they can improve in their job roles. However, you must observe that we are not only talking about annual reviews or appraisals here. Instead, many organizations need a healthy, open culture where people give and receive feedback regularly.[2]

It helps make important decisions

Effective feedback is very helpful, both positive and negative. It offers valuable information useful for making critical decisions. It is a norm in top-performing companies because they consistently look

---

[2] *WHY FEEDBACK IS IMPORTANT IN THE WORKPLACE, Retrieved from* https://www.t-three.com/soak/insights/why-feedback-is-important

for ways to make themselves even better. Continuous improvement is not just a catchphrase for top-performing companies. They focus on the feedback obtained from across the entire organization, including clients, suppliers, employees, customers, stakeholders, and vendors. They take into account each one of these. These companies are not only good at accepting feedback; they deliberately ask for it. They know it can help highlight their strengths and weaknesses and help make decisions.

It Helps Motivate and Improve Performance

Providing feedback motivates employees to perform better than expected. They like to feel appreciated and valued and being asked to provide feedback can help formulate business decisions. Feedback is often mistaken for criticism when, in fact, constructive feedback can help improve performance and increase productivity.

Feedback Is A Tool for Continued Learning

To remain aligned with the business' goals, continued feedback across the organization is essential. It helps create strategies and develop new products and services for a better outcome. It also helps improve relationships within and outside the organization. The key to improvement is continued learning, which is only possible through regular feedback. Hence, invest time in asking and learning about how others interact with your organization.[3]

Elements of Constructive Feedback

Now that you know the importance of giving feedback, it is imperative that you also know about the elements of constructive feedback. Giving constructive feedback to employees can be

---

[3] *5 Reasons Why Feedback is Important, Retrieved from* https://www.snapsurveys.com/blog/5-reasons-feedback-important/

daunting for many managers. In fact, managers often say it is the least favorite part of their job. Being able to do so effectively can have a long-lasting impact on your employees.

There are chances that your employees are doing their job quite well, and only certain areas require improvements. It can be tempting to let things slide until it is time to review their performance. However, it is not always healthy. A small session of constructive feedback conducted regularly can save a lengthy and uncomfortable performance review later. You can also expect an increase in their performance by tackling the issue at an early stage. To communicate your ideas constructively, it is essential to get your ideas across in the most effective way. It would be best if you found a way to give constructive feedback without being detrimental. You aim to boost the self-confidence of your employees instead of blowing their self-confidence sky-high. Here's what you need to know.

Be Specific

Beating around the bush has never resulted in fruitful consequences, no matter the communication style. Get to the point and stick to it. There are chances that your feedback can be misunderstood if you are vague, and your employee might continue to make the same mistakes without realizing it.

Outline the exact instance to your employees where they had trouble or made a mistake and ask them how they can do the same task differently. If necessary, create notes with specific examples of the incidents. This will help you handle the issue effectively and get the message across. Perhaps, you need to do a little retraining to walk them through the right steps. Remember to be as authentic and transparent as possible. When training or leading others, it became necessary to correct an action. One of the tools in my teaching toolbox was to share my experiences if I had similar problems or challenges or see this challenge in others. It is good for the employee to know they are not alone in mistakes or lessons learned.

Be Timely

This is a vital step in giving corrective feedback. You must learn how to give prompt feedback while the incident is still fresh in everyone's mind. The effectiveness of teaching in the moment will be at stake if you take too long to point out the error and what your employee did the best.

They will also be able to associate your feedback with their action if you provide them with an immediate response. They are likelier to retain the feedback, learn from it, and think twice if they find themselves in the same situation.

Be Positive

You must include positive feedback for all the negative ones you give out. This brings up a good point; when you are giving corrective or constructive feedback, for that matter, use the formula of *Good-Bad-Good*. Tell them something good that they did, or you noticed, share the mistake or "bad" news, and then close on something good once again.

Focus on your employees' strengths and allow them to be part of the solution instead of you emphasize or come up with the solutions. This is a great way also to teach the co-worker how to develop critical thinking skills.

Again, if you need to prepare notes for their strengths and areas that need improvement, do it. This is a time where the co-worker may feel embarrassed or even guilty for making a mistake. Focus on building self-esteem and continuously encourage growth and learning. Tell them what measures you are willing to take as a leader to help your employees perform better. You have some responsibility here too. This is where the employee needs your leadership; their problem is your problem. It can be beneficial if you set a time for review for a week or two, so they have a clear timeframe for getting up to expectations. Assure them that you are available at any time of the day if they need further assistance or have questions related to anything. This can also motivate them not to give up on the process. Plan on spot checks throughout the day for the first couple of days and reinforce corrected performance.

Be Understanding

Get to the root of the issue and discuss what he or she could have done instead. Most times, supervisors just want to tell workers what to do. One of the methods I often use is, 'tell me why this happened, or tell me the way it happened, or tell me how the oversight happened.' This allows me to understand what the co-worker was thinking and uncover their misunderstandings or even an initial training issue.

Always discuss challenges transparently. Offer them help where they might need it and work with them to figure out if any extra assistance is needed with knowledge or skill development. When you take this approach, you may even be surprised by ideas co-workers have to improve systems and procedures. Use this time of feedback as a learning opportunity for both; you and the employee.[4]

Demonstrate the Qualities You Want to See in Others

Before you approach your employees about the areas that might need improvement, make sure you are not making the same mistakes. Employees are likelier to respect your criticism and

---

[4] 4 Vital Elements of giving Constructive Feedback, Retrieved from https://collegeforadultlearning.edu.au/4-vital-elements-of-giving-constructive-feedback/

It Can Be Constructive or Corrective

corrective feedback when you are a living example of your own expectations. For instance, if a specific employee has anger issues and finds it challenging to control their temper, make sure you have control over your emotions in the workplace. This could be a modeled behavior from watching your approach. Back in my earlier days, I was not the best of leaders. I was very egotistical and thought the workforce was there for me. I truly had a, "I'm the boss" mentality. One day, it came time for me to give corrective action to a member of the workforce. For the purposes of this story, we will call the employee Yancy. Yancy was a brass gentleman, a bull in a china shop. He was great as his job but did not know how to communicate with people very well. He had an interaction with another co-worker and made some inappropriate comments that needed his action addressed. When Yancy came to my office, his corrective action was already completed and ready for me to administer it. Boy, did I read Yancy the riot act. My tone was direct and to the point, I allowed my emotions to dictate my actions, made some comments that I should not have said as I tried to get my point across. At the end of my tirade, Yancy asked one question that straightened me up and shook me, "how is the way you are talking to me any different than what I said and did?" I had no response, just looking into his face as my mind made sense of the body slam I just received. He was correct, I was just as guilty as he was in his situation. Yancy did not receive corrective action that day and together, we agreed to learn how best to communicate with other people. I began reading emotional intelligence articles, sending them to Yancy, he would also send me things to read. It was an interesting learning lesson for both of us. The lesson I took from this great example was, talk to people as you want to be talked to.

Make the Right Choice of Words

Make sure that you do not use the words 'always' or 'never.' These words can prompt them to speak up in their defense. For instance, when talking to your employee about their attendance, do not say, *"You are always late."* This statement will make them feel the need to defend themselves against the accusation and look for occasions when they were on time. Instead, you can say, *"I have noticed that you have been late for the past three days. This can be disruptive for the team."* Believe me; it will turn out to be a far more productive discussion.

Give the Other Person A Chance to Respond

After you are done explaining your point of view and the amendments you would like to see in their work, give them a chance to respond. Sometimes, perceptions are not realistic, and it is important to remember this. There is a possibility of external factors affecting their performance that you were not aware of.

Moreover, allow the employee to brainstorm how they can improve the situation moving forward. Allow them to participate in the conversation instead of just being the listener. Inspire them to follow through on the discussion, and you will see how they can considerably improve in a short time.

Take Time to Be Reflective

Constructive feedback motivates employees to work more efficiently and meet your expectations, especially when you are knowledgeable about the situation and willing to provide timely feedback. It also gives you an insight into how you can improve yourself in managing your employees every day, think about what you can do to keep them motivated, and what additional training they may require. You can come up with incentives or give awards for achieving goals.

Providing your team with constructive feedback can help them overcome their weaknesses and improve their performance. It will inspire them in a number of ways and motivate them to do better continually. How you guide your organization forward is a crucial part of being a leader. It is your responsibility to transform negative behaviors into positive ones. If you follow through with these guidelines, nothing can stop you from flourishing as a strong coach.[5] More importantly, you are creating stronger workers.

How Can Feedback Prevent Employees from Improving?

However, there are also times when feedback prevents employees from improving. It is usually due to some psychological factors. How do you react when someone at work asks you, *"Can I give you some feedback?"* I can bet if you are like most professionals, tension will start to take over your system. You begin to prepare yourself to hear how you have screwed up your work.

As the negative thoughts run through your mind, you start to worry about the consequences. What if it stops you from getting that promotion? Or even worse, maybe, have you put your job at stake? It is a sign that your brain is directing itself into the survival mode, in which it stops all the other functions and focuses specifically on getting away from the risk right in front of you.

Yes, it means that our brains perceive getting feedback at work as being chased by a dog on the street. You run for your life, and it follows you until you can sneak out of its sight. This is the reason why most people are resistant to feedback from co-workers and fail to improve.

---

[5] *Four Key Elements for Offering Constructive Criticism Successfully , Retrieved from* https://www.sandler.com/blog/four-key-elements-offering-constructive-criticism-successfully/

It is sad to see that most people cannot receive constructive criticism without feeling a wave of anxiety inside their bodies. When you are in the moment, your brain does not know whether you are getting a piece of feedback or are in a situation of life and death. It only focuses on responding to the perceived danger.

Now, look at this situation from the perspective of the one giving feedback. Let's say their goal and intention was only to improve the person's performance. They may be coming from a genuinely good place, wanting to help the other person. However, that does not mean the other person is ready to receive their criticism in the same way.

They might begin to wonder whether you are sympathetic or nosy. Their body begins to prepare itself for the intense physical threat. Under such circumstances, the person's ability to thoughtfully receive the feedback turns off, and their brains cannot handle any shared information.

This is why giving critical feedback has very little or no relation to improving the intended person's performance. Though they look fine on the outside, their brain is not in the right state to adequately accept, process, and consider the improvements offered by the respective person. It is because their brain is busy working on a single task to escape the situation.

More Positive Feedback Isn't the Answer, Either

People have this visceral negative reaction to feedback because we have trained our brains to believe that all feedback is critical and never positive. At least, some surveys have resulted in this possibility. The answer is to counterbalance your criticism by giving out a ton of positive feedback, to teach them that not all feedback is created equal and that you also see all the good things they do.

It Can Be Constructive or Corrective

However, there's also a possibility that leaders are not giving out enough positive feedback. According to research, 61% of employees report that they have not received any positive recognition at work in at least six months, if ever. It is as if it's so rare that many employees rate the importance of positive recognition and appreciation higher than their desire for more money.

So yes, do give out positive feedback, but you also must be careful with this tactic. You need to give positive feedback 2 to 1 to effectively balance negative ones and maintain a productive relationship with your employees. That is a lot of work to do, but it is the only way to make improvements and help them take criticism to improve.[6]

> *"Criticism, like rain, should be gentle enough to nourish a man's growth without destroying his roots."*
> **-Frank A. Clark**

What Is Corrective Feedback?

Let's switch gears. Corrective feedback is information provided to individuals or groups about how others perceive their behavior and actions and how it may affect them. Corrective feedback should always be delivered to bring positive change, which is a need.

Corrective feedback is an essential element in every organization. The leader is responsible for letting people know where they are and where the organization wants them to be. Employees must understand what is expected of them in terms of goals and objectives.

---

[6] *Why Giving Feedback At Work Doesn't Improve Performance, And What You Can Do About It, Retrieved from,* https://www.forbes.com/sites/karlynborysenko/2019/03/19/why-giving-feedback-at-work-doesnt-improve-performance-and-what-you-can-do-about-it/#407691d329ba

Corrective feedback is a useful tool for indicating if things are going in the right direction or a problem that needs to be addressed. Your objective in giving feedback is to provide guidance by supplying information in a useful manner, either by supporting productive behavior or guiding someone back on track to deliver a successful performance. Therefore, it comes with positive intentions.

Purpose of Corrective Feedback

The goal of corrective feedback is to enhance the personal growth of individuals and create a culture that is understood in your organization. Here are a few goals of giving corrective feedback
- To help individuals in their personal development.
- To decrease the confusion regarding expectations and ongoing performance.
- To improve communication among individuals and groups.
- To improve relationships among team members and different teams.
- To help employees improve their performance.
- To increase the effectiveness of an activity or initiative.
- To improve the mood within an organization.[7]

Constructive vs. Corrective Feedback

Constructive feedback can be motivating and makes people feel good. It can tell the person they are doing well, while corrective feedback tells them about the areas where they are not doing well and need improvement.

Constructive feedback helps establish trust in the person giving feedback as someone who values and understands the employee's

---

[7] Section 4. Providing Corrective Feedback https://ctb.ku.edu/en/table-of-contents/advocacy/encouragement-education/corrective-feedback/main

contribution. Whereas corrective feedback can be upsetting for people, and consequently, they often become defensive and demotivated. However, corrective feedback provides specific areas where they should change. Thus, it can be the most effective in terms of helping people improve. At the same time, too much corrective feedback can be demotivating. It can create an impression that the person giving feedback is unfairly negative or is only out there to get an employee.

So, you must be very careful with corrective feedback as it can severely impact an employee's performance and engagement. There is a thin line between positive corrective feedback and a negative one. Moreover, if you are not careful, it can easily be crossed.[8]

Consequently, it's better to give constructive feedback because it never fails to motivate the employees. You can easily tell them the required areas of improvement under this feedback without offending them. For that, you need to learn the right way of giving corrective feedback, keeping in mind all the elements of effective corrective feedback.

Elements of Corrective Feedback

Here are the elements of corrective feedback that you must know before you go out and speak to your employees.

Give Positive and Negative Feedback

For feedback to be effective, it must be well received. But you will be surprised to know that way too many people only provide negative feedback and fail to point out the positives. Many managers also deliver negative feedback in a harmful manner. Therefore, you

---

[8] Kinds of Feedback, Retrieved from, https://www.careerwave.me/coaching-tool/kinds-of-feedback/

must make sure that the person taking the feedback is open to listening.

You can create an environment that promotes growth from mistakes if you have a history of giving out both: the positives and the negatives. The tool that can play a crucial role here is to make the employee or the person receiving feedback feel appreciated and valued. This, of course, requires emotional intelligence, so a leader should have this quality.

The right way is to keep the negatives and positives as balanced as possible, as providing negative feedback only makes the whole process less effective. You do not want to offend the recipient and focusing only on the negatives may make them feel that you are just being critical as you always are. This can immensely reduce feedback's impact, so you need to change your approach. Look for ways you can praise your employee's performance while offering them avenues for improvement.

Always Start with the Positive

It may be a dead horse since we have covered it already, but it cannot be overstated enough, to create an environment where feedback is received and processed well, you must always begin with the positives. It lowers the recipient's defenses, and they will pay more attention to whatever you have to say about their work. Once you have started the conversation positively, you can easily begin to discuss what you may have done differently.

Focus on the Behavior, NOT on the Person

Do not use the word, 'You.' Avoid it as much as you can. For instance, please do not say you did this or that wrong as it is too personal. It can offend the other person and shuts the communication down. Focus on the behavior or work product instead. You can begin with, "I might have done it differently." This approach is way more effective.

Explain WHY It Matters

It is essential to focus on the consequences of the mistakes, the reasons why you needed to correct them before it's too late. When you explain the importance of the error, it automatically makes space for improvements. It does have an impact on you, the firm, the client, and the organization as a whole. When you explain the consequences, it is evident why you needed to point it out in the first place. Real-life scenarios can be best in explaining this. It also brings to the surface that you were not only feeding your ego, but the matter is actually serious and requires your attention.

Don't Wait

For corrective feedback to be effective, you must give it out in close time to the error. Take the time to do it, no matter how busy you are! Do not put off talking about what happened for more than a day. Waiting to talk is much less effective.

Ignoring the mistake made will not make things any better. The associate needs to be informed of their poor performance, which creates poor morale. Hence, when you point it out at the right time and let them know about their poor performance all along the way, they are hopefully more accepting and willing to transition themselves into a better version.

Assume a Positive Intent

Always assume that the person had good intentions. Generally, no one wishes to screw up on purpose. So always approach it as an honest mistake with no ill intentions. If you approach the recipient as having done their best under the circumstances, you will also open up a dialogue for discussion. Be firm yet compassionate in delivering your message. Set up the environment for positive and constructive communication.

Take the Receiver's Perspective under Consideration

Always end the conversation by asking the receiver about your feedback for their take on the situation. You can be wrong in your criticism. Use this session as an opportunity for you to grow and learn, as well. Be honest and admit to the receiver if you were wrong, same as I had to do with Yancy. This builds credibility and trust between you two. Being humble and honest is the key. Believe me, your colleagues will appreciate you even more.

Everyone Wants Feedback, Including You!

Whether it is at work or in personal lives, everyone wants feedback. Think about it for a moment. You want to know that you are appreciated, right? Knowing that feedback is wanted empowers you to provide more feedback in a timely and effective manner. You must create an environment where you are open and active with your employees. This makes it easier for you to provide feedback, no matter if it is positive or negative. Being able to communicate openly is an essential factor in learning how to be an effective leader.[9]

Remember: Positive Communication is Powerful

I know I keep hitting on this component, but I cannot stress the importance of this step. The way you express yourself affects the other person, whether your message is received positively or negatively. This also has a significant influence on the likely

---

[9] 9 Critical Components of Constructive Feedback, Retrieved from https://attorneyexecutivecoaching.com/9-critical-components-of-constructive-feedback/

response. Even when you are conveying unwelcomed news, the impact can be softened by using positive language.

The first step is to be aware of whether the phrasing and language you are using are positive or negative. This is not an easy task when you are primarily focused on finding the right vocabulary. Therefore, make it a habit to always speak positively. The impact and the results of this one habit will amaze you. It will be your most vital tool when it comes to giving feedback. Hence, as a leader, you must know the difference between constructive and corrective feedback. It is the only way your organization and team can learn and grow positively.

*"We all need people who will give us feedback. That's how we improve." -**Bill Gates***

CHAPTER 4

COACHING VS. PROGRESSIVE DISCIPLINE

Part of your responsibility when leading others is taking the necessary steps to change and improve employee performance or behavior. There can be different ways to go about accomplishing this goal. Typically, most organizations use the method of progressive discipline to obtain this objective. Although progressive discipline is not meant to be a punishment for an employee, that is precisely how most managers and organizations use it. However, this chapter intends to change your view on how best to deal with employee's job-related behavior.

The Process

The progressive discipline process includes a series of increasingly formal efforts to provide feedback to the employee to correct the problem. The goal of progressive discipline is to get the employee's attention, so they understand that performance improvement is needed to remain productive, continue on a good path, and, truthfully, stay employed.

One of the first things I look at when consulting with organizations is their employee engagement success and their use of the progressive discipline process. It is interesting to hear an organization's philosophy on the best way to dole out the chain of discipline.

To be successful as a coach, it is vital to move away from this antiquated method of changing behavior and instead develop a culture of growing the workforce through coaching. Let's suppose you are not familiar with the progressive discipline process. In that case, it is an organizational policy with a well-defined series of corrective action steps that will be taken when a worker violates work policies, procedures, or established rules. The progression of discipline usually follows these steps:

Verbal Warning

A verbal warning is an informal one by nature. It ensures that the employee is aware of the infraction and is given the opportunity to take the necessary steps to remedy it (the warning is verbal, but you should document it with all the pertinent information from the discussion).

Written Warning (One Or More)

A written warning is a formal documented warning to the employee. It usually is issued if the verbal warning does not result in a positive change in the employee's performance or behavior. Written warnings can also be used if there is a new work performance issue that warrants jumping right to a written warning. This step usually includes an action plan or the next steps that must be taken to ensure that there are no further consequences. An employer may choose to issue more than one written warning for the same or different infractions. Usually, the employer and employee sign the written warning, and it goes into the employee's personnel file.

Suspension (With or Without Pay)

Suspension is commonly reserved for major infractions or conditions that require investigation before further action is taken. It can serve as a final warning to the employee that the termination will result next if their behavior is not improved.

Termination

Termination is usually a last resort, but sometimes, it cannot be avoided. Documentation is essential every step of the way, but especially for any termination decision.

Bear in mind that some infractions may warrant skipping the early steps in the progressive discipline process altogether. Having a progressive disciplinary system does not mean that an employer cannot immediately move to termination of severe violations, such as physical violence, harassment, theft, or significant safety issues. These infractions should be explained in the organizational policy upfront.

The Drawbacks of Progressive Discipline

Since I am not a fan of the progressive discipline process, I will not be discussing the pros of instilling this program into an organization. In fact, it is my mission to change this old-fashioned system of correcting performance issues by using a coaching methodology instead. But, with that said, here are some cons:

It is inflexible

Such a policy can seem inflexible. HR and managers must make judgment calls about deviating from the progressive steps, as may be necessary when considering all circumstances.

It can cause discrimination

Disciplinary actions could appear to be biased if not followed consistently for every employee. Remember, this problem can occur at any time. Various disciplinary actions are often taken for different employees who have committed the same violation. It is not unique to employers using progressive discipline. The primary concern here is the potential for litigation if this type of unfairness or favoritism occurs.

It brings fear to the work environment

Leaders use a fear factor when it comes to wielding the progressive discipline policy. Using it as an iron fist implies that all the steps will and must be followed before any termination occurs. This could change the belief or imply a contract that exists, stating that an employee will never be terminated without these steps. It is why members of the workforce fear that progressive discipline is a punishment and used as such.

Time-consuming

This process can be time-consuming if executed correctly, especially for organizations with limited resources. Not only does the process itself take time, but leaders need to be trained in the proper delivery as well. Leaders must know that prior to issuing discipline, documenting each incidence is vital, and having appropriate follow-up is paramount.

Non-practical

For some businesses, especially smaller organizations, it may not be practical to follow these steps. It may not be practical to keep an employee on the payroll who violates any rule, and termination may seem more realistic. Or it may not be practical to keep the business running with a suspended employee. It just might not be beneficial to implement this program in every organization.

Managers typically seem to take an undesirable approach toward that particular employee once discipline has been given out. Simply put, the employee that just received a link in the chain of the progressive discipline process needs your leadership more than ever. Instead, in my experience, supervisors and managers shun the employee because of their unacceptable behavior.

This behavior by the leaders of an organization only alienates the employee further from the organizational community, leading to other behavioral issues. Therefore, it is essential for you as a leader to take care of this one crucial step to inspire and motivate the employee. Remember, as I said earlier, you want to improve their performance rather than further pushing them away from the mission and vision of the organization.

The New Paradigm

In today's constantly growing world, we must develop a new paradigm in every aspect of our lives, whether in our home or in the workplace. When it comes to developing a new paradigm in building a strong workforce with performance improvement, the progressive discipline process sits on the negative side of developing higher employee engagement.

So, how about considering the positive side, beginning with respect? A progressive discipline process is a power-based approach for developing a hierarchical relationship with the workforce. Remember, we talked about constructive feedback and how it is better than corrective feedback. The same rule implies in this situation. Consider, we need our workforce to achieve organizational success. We go through the hiring process and invite the chosen candidate into our organization to assist in that objective. We need our workforce more than they need us. When we hire employees, they come to us with a set of skills, knowledge, and experience. The goal of a leader must be to grow their employees' skills, knowledge, and expertise to ensure that the organization continues to grow.

This is where coaching is paramount as a developed work culture. Most of the time, it's not the case. Managers will have more of the approach that the workforce is there for the manager, rather than the manager serving the workforce, which is utterly wrong. We need to coach them instead of making them feel as though they are only there to serve and not learn. Remember the golden rule of life: it's always about the give and take.

> *"Coaching is unlocking a person's potential to maximize their own performance. It is helping them to learn rather than teaching them." -**John Whitmore***

There is detailed research that outlines a connection between employee engagement, productivity, resourcefulness, retention, and delivering a high degree of customer service. What is the best way to achieve this? A great question! It starts with developing a culture where the employees feel respected by all leaders and their coworkers.

This type of respected culture ensures a foundation of strong physical, psychological, and emotional well-being of all members of the workforce. It also helps motivate them to bring their best to work and provide them with a sense of belonging. It also means that you will not always need to give them feedback, as they would already know where they need improvements. When your employees start to feel that their contributions matter, that is when you know that you are winning.

Coaching Vs. Progressive Discipline

Now with that being said, as I mentioned earlier, employees, when hired, have a specific set of skills and experience they bring when joining your organization. It is the leaders' responsibility to help them improve and grow those skills to the next level. Sometimes, these new and present employees fall short of meeting the required expectations. That is when coaching must be conducted.

When handled correctly, conducting a coaching session can help set up the required goals, lead to changed behavior, and develop a blueprint for needed growth potential. However, some things need to be taken care of and specific guidelines that must be followed. Conducting a coaching session should include the following essentials:

Identify the challenge or performance gap

This is the difference between the expectation of performance and the actual employee performance. That's how you identify the challenge and the points you must work on. When I was a supervisor, I watched an employee perform a totally subpar task to our expectations. Let's call this employee Jim.

Jim needed to be talked to, and his behavior definitely required changing too. I remember thinking Jim would be cancer and toxic to the workforce because of him skipping steps and not following the proper procedures. Not only did I label Jim cancer, but I also voiced this opinion with my peers. In the counseling session, I outlined what I saw, my poor opinion of Jim, and my intent to give them a written corrective action. I was feeling pretty good about correcting this behavior and teaching Jim a valuable lesson.

However, Jim totally sunk my battleship with a little piece of information (I was getting visions of my Yancy interaction all over again, and yes I made a similar mistake here too). He mentioned that he had been doing this task since he started with the organization about six months ago. This piece of information made my position stronger until Jim told me Sean trained him, a Field Training Officer we fired about four months ago for some of the same failures of following the proper procedure. Instead of investigating and determining Jim's challenge, I jumped to conclusions and found him guilty. This was a total failure on my part of being an advocate for Jim.

Before jumping to conclusions and labeling Jim as cancer, the lesson was I should have done some investigating.

Observed Behavior

I should have immediately talked to Jim and shared what I observed that particular day. I could have saved myself a lot of embarrassment by only saying, *"Jim, I saw you go into a home the other day without the proper equipment. As a Paramedic, it is essential to bring in the appropriate equipment for every call."* This would have enabled Jim to give me his back story about being trained by Sean instead of all the scenes I created that embarrassed both of us.

Expectation of Behavior

In this scenario, Jim's performance was only a logical result of inadequate training during his orientation. If we concluded this was a failure or over-sightedness on Jim's part, it would have been appropriate for me to share what the expectations were and what needed to be Jim's process now, as he moved forward.

Build trust and assurance

When an employee discusses a performance issue, it is crucial to make this meeting as non-threatening as possible. It is your responsibility to create an environment that will reinforce your relationship of trust, service, and respect for their performance. Your approach will instill the assurance that you are committed to the employee's growth and not there to be a hammer. This will assist the employee in feeling comfortable and be less defensive. When employees know that they made an honest mistake, and we are trying to help them grow, they become more open. Sometimes, coaching sessions must be more formal, and documentation of the session needs to be completed and signed by the manager and employee. This is where using a Performance Improvement Plan (PIP) works quite well.

When conducting a formal coaching session, follow these steps:

Prepare for the Coaching Session

Every time you are preparing to coach an employee, take some time to prepare for the conversation. Your workforce is the most vital component to your success as a leader. You are trying to get the very best out of that workforce. This preparation is an essential component of the upcoming coaching session.

To keep the conversation respectful, make sure you are in the proper mindset and know how you want the conversation to flow. This is also a two-way conversation, and you cannot command its flow. Remember my mistake above with Jim? Don't you think it was quite unprofessional of me to label Jim as a cancer? Therefore, avoid labeling and using unprofessional words like cancer, lazy, or poor performer. This is the very reason why you need to prepare for the coaching session.

Determine the Cause

This is a significant aspect of coaching. It is vital that you determine the cause of the troubling behavior and why it occurred.

Use guiding questions to determine the root of the problem. It is also essential to use open-ended questions and turn the conversation over to the employee. Ask questions like, *"Why do you think this occurred?" "What is causing this?" "Is there something getting in your way?"* Or *"What's going on?"* This is a great way to start a discussion and allow the employee to tell you the real problem.

As a practice, remember that the first answer rarely ever gets to the underlying issue. It is appropriate to continue to probe and guide the conversation with questions like, *"Tell me more?"* And *"Help me understand?"* This signifies that you are actually listening, and you are engaged in the conversation. Remember, this is a discussion, and you are there to listen and facilitate, not dictate.

Do Not Provide Resolutions, Facilitate Them

For this to be a successful coaching session, the employee must outline the resolutions and how they will fix the issue. In short, this is not your problem to solve. You are two professionals who are adults. One adult has an issue, and you are trying to facilitate a change in their behavior or performance. For this to be successful, the employee must take ownership of their issue. One of the best questions to ask is, *"Now that we know the root cause, how can you address that?"*

When the employee is responsible for developing a solution, they will be committed and empowered to hold true to their word of correcting and changing the challenge. This is the best way to witness a significant change in no time.

Document the Conversation

With the employee still in the room, fill out the appropriate sections of the PIP, taking a good account of the challenge, the root cause, and the resolution. Another crucial factor is to determine

Coaching vs. Progressive Discipline

a timeline for the behavior or performance issue to be corrected. Once that has been documented, both the manager and employee should sign the document.

A copy should be given to the employee. One of the final steps is to share some motivational and inspirational words of encouragement to end this discussion. You should also plan a time for a follow-up to check in on the progress in reaching this listed goal. Below is a sample PIP for your consideration.

Performance Improvement Plan (PIP)

For: John Smith
Area Needing Improvement: Late to Work

Performance Challenge: Recognizing John has had 3 tardies in 1 week

Plan for Improvement – John mentioned that he has been having trouble getting around in traffic secondary to construction. His normal route to work has been bogged down with more traffic than normal. John has come up with the following solutions:
- Leave a bit earlier
- Find an alternative route
- Call his supervisor if he is going to be late

Time for Improvement: John states he will begin this practice tomorrow and give his word he will rectify this challenge as quickly as possible

Failure to meet PIP: Continued coaching sessions will be needed to fix this challenge if not corrected. It is vital that all employees be on time so not to disrupt the rest of the team's processes on beginning the day.

Notes: _____
_____
_____
_____
_____

Chris Cebollero 2/17/2021   John Smith   2/17/2021
―――――――――――――――   ―――――――――――――――
Supervisor Signature   Date   Employee Signature   Date

Sometimes coaching does not work

Sometimes, initial coaching sessions do not work, and you must conduct additional sessions. This second discussion should move along the same path as the first, focusing on facilitation.

An additional dialogue will go along the lines of why the employee did not hold up their end of the bargain. Remember, the employee identified the problem, determined why it occurred, and developed a resolution with a timeframe to fix the shortcoming. Failure of this process falls squarely on the shoulders of the employee.

As a leader, this conversation needs to be sterner and direct. This is where the discussion about being definitive with fixing the problem must take place. The manager will need to set a strict timetable for resolving the issue and develop a schedule for progress checks.

Failure to correct this problem after subsequent check-in sessions and the appropriate time limit may result in additional training, reduced duties, or even ending the professional relationship.

In a nutshell, the progressive discipline process kills morale and causes poor employee engagement, satisfaction, and productivity. Developing a culture of coaching shows that you are focused on employee growth. On the other hand, it also shows the employee that they are respected, seen as adults, and dealt with professionally. It gives the message that the leadership and workforce will work together to grow the employee to the next level.

CHAPTER 5

MOTIVATE AND INSPIRE THE WORKFORCE

"An employee's motivation is a direct result of the sum of interactions with his or her manager."
-Bob Nelson

No matter what aspect of life you are looking at, you need motivation. Motivation starts from the very beginning of the day once the alarm goes off. Throughout the day, motivation is needed to complete job-related tasks, work on short and long-term goals, and get yourself from where you are today to where you wish to be tomorrow.

As a leader and coach, it is vital you learn the skills needed to develop a culture of inspiration and motivation for those you are guiding. In this chapter, let's outline some of the best practices for fostering motivation.

Motivation is the true secret sauce in cultivating a high degree of employee engagement, satisfaction, and higher productivity.

When you are able to inspire and motivate, you are now opening a door that will allow you to build the strongest workforce possible.

Motivation can come from a variety of sources. It can come from wanting to achieve a specific goal, get to the next level of your career, or it comes from the enjoyment of the work itself.

One of the biggest points that need to be discussed first is as coaches, we cannot motivate anyone. Motivation has to be intrinsic, meaning it has to come from inside of the individual. A great leader and coach cultivates an environment and break down barriers that will allow inspiration and motivation to flourish.

Our first step down the rabbit hole of developing a culture of motivation starts with taking into account two main obstacles that hinder workers" success: their fears.

Fear of Failure

The first and most major obstacle is the fear of failure. This fear is one of the biggest barriers to the achievement of success in adults. Think about it a minute: when we are in a professional role, the fear of failure is paralyzing. As professionals, we want to do a good job, create a name for ourselves, and develop a solid professional reputation. Yet, when we think about why people won't come outside their comfort zone or refuse to take risks or put themselves out there in any way, it is because the fear of failure is so stifling. Individuals would rather live-in obscurity than take a leap of faith. Your job as a coach is to set up that airbag at the bottom when they decide to jump.

The next obstacle is the fear of rejection, which also encompasses feeling disapproval, and not being considered a part of the team or organization. Part of the organizational socialization elements is when the job is offered and knowing you are going to be part of an organization. You hope there will be a great teamwork culture, being able to fit in, and maybe even make friends. Those with low self-confidence or low self-esteem may not want to interact with the team in fear of being rejected by the team for poor performance.

Regardless of the reasons these fears populate, they are there, and leaders have to prepare to assist their team members in facing them and, more importantly, overcoming them. Coaching individuals will not occur if they are secretly harboring these monsters that are preparing to sabotage any success.

Outlining expectations

Believe it or not, one of the first things to be considered in developing a culture of motivation is outlining a clear set of expectations for all positions within the organization and the understanding that there will be accountability to those expectations. This is the level playing field that everyone is measured and grows from. When outlining expectations, follow these tips:

1. Setting clear goals and objectives for every position based on job responsibilities and the skills needed to master that particular position.
2. Ensure that there is a clear expectation that outlines metrics that needs to be measured, and how that metric fits into the overall responsibility of the bigger picture. It is paramount that the team knows why the task is important or why it needs to be measured.
3. Set the expectation of what excellent performance looks like. Think about it; you can just do the minimum requirement, do more than what is required, and of course, overachieve and excel. If we do not want the bare minimum from our employees, we must begin with the expectation of what excellent performance looks like.
4. Now that you have laid out expectations, the next step is to set time aside weekly or monthly for coaching sessions

related to performance and reaching goals. This is what we do as leaders, or should I say, this is what leaders should be doing on a regular basis. It never really happens that way because we have our own workload and have meetings every 45 seconds, but you have to make this a priority.

5. Develop a merit or reward system for outstanding work, achievements, and a job well done. It could be a lunch, a free coffee, or just a plain old simple pat on the back. Everyone wants to know they are doing great work; what will be your process for sharing that it was a job well done?

Benefits of A Motivated Workforce

As we now begin developing an environment that grows an inspired and motivated workforce, let's look at what happens when the workforce is highly motivated. It can provide several advantages.

1. Increased Efficiency

When we outline the efficiency of the team member it should not only be based on their capability or experience. Members of our workforce come to us with a set of skills and experiences that we as coaches have to polish and grow. As leaders, we are getting work done through other people, and we have to ensure we are getting the very best out of those members. This is why it is so important to get a good balance between the ability to do the job and the willingness to want to perform that job to the best of their ability. When this occurs, you will have an increased productivity with an outcome of excellence.

2. Lower levels of staff turnover

If employees do not want to come to work, it is hard to get the mission of reaching the vision completed. When you develop a motivated workforce, it helps you keep high-performing employees. I have worked in some organizations that have had an attrition rate of over 30% in my career. On top of losing employees, we were not able to recruit their replacement. Here is a secret, I am going to whisper this so come closer to the page. The best way to stop poor recruitment is to have high retention. It sounds simple, but it's true that you have no issue recruiting if you keep your highly engaged workforce. When you have a high retention of your team, this will lower initial training costs and helps grow the company's reputation in the market.

3. Lower levels of absenteeism

Another big problem is employees that abuse their sick leave. Somewhere in all of our careers, there have been "mental health" sick days. I'm sure you have heard the joke of the employee that couldn't go to work because he had an eye problem. They could not see themselves coming into work today. When you have an environment that is toxic or not a positive place to work, you will have tons of call-offs. When your workforce is motivated, when they feel appreciated, when you are investing in their professional development, they will want to be there.

4. Increased employee commitment

Employees will generally put their best efforts into their tasks when they are fully motivated to perform them. This shows an increased level of commitment.

5. Improved employee satisfaction

Employee satisfaction can lead to positive growth for the company. Hence, it is crucial for every company.

6. Ongoing employee development

This can be taken a couple of different ways, and they are all true. First, a strong culture of motivation in the organization will facilitate workers in wanting to set and, more importantly, reach personal goals. This allows the employee to realize the clear link between effort and results once that worker meets some initial goals, which will further motivate them to continue at a higher level.

Another way this works in employee development is the building of a strong, cohesive team. Motivated workers respect their teammates and want to do well for overall team performance. This assists in developing a stable work environment of each other and will grow an attitude of both flexibility and adaptability.

7. World-Class Organization

When co-workers are inspired and motivated, it equates to satisfaction and engagement, leading to higher productivity. More importantly, it grows the reputation of the organization. Who wouldn't want to achieve a World Series or Super Bowl ring? Of course, this is hard to come by, yet we can work for a world-class organization. Through hard work, dedication, and commitment, that is a team that we can be on and win with. When this level of motivation takes hold on an organization it is likely to improve product quality or the customer service associated with a product, which, in turn, has a positive impact on the organization's reputation.[10]

---

[10] People Management: Introduction to Motivation (GCSE) Retrieved from https://www.tutor2u.net/business/reference/people-management-introduction-tomotivation#:~:text=A%20well%2Dmotivated%20workforce%20can,(amount%20produced%20per%20employee).&text=Lower%20levels%20of%20absenteeism%20as,of%20employees%20leaving%20the%20business).

How to Increase Employee Motivation

Now that we laid out why motivation should be a strong focal point to your coaching skills toolbox, here are the three best practices that will help you increase employee motivation in your workplace.

1. Improve communication

The easiest way to increase employee motivation is by having multiple positive communication strategies inside the workplace. It is important to have one official mode of communication and a few other methods as well. Social media allows a platform for some organizations; closed Facebook pages are a great unofficial way to share information and get the word out.

Obviously, nothing takes the place of good old-fashioned leadership briefings. This is even easier than before, with the ability to send podcasts or even video messages. A quick tip, when using audio or video messaging, don't be so stuffy; allow your personality to come through and let the workforce hear you on a personal level.

When possible, try setting aside some time each day to talk with employees, or you can join them during coffee breaks instead of sitting at your desk. Your desk is where you work; it is not where you lead or coach from. You actually make employees feel as though you are part of the team by doing so. This small act makes you a leader instead of just being the "boss".

When it comes to communication, there is nothing more important than listening to members of your workforce. Employees also want the organization they are working at to flourish and do better and win that Super Bowl ring. Many may have excellent ideas, ranging from operational improvements to money-saving enhancements. When employees are motivated, these ideas will flow, and you as their leader must make an effort to take some time to ask and listen to suggestions.

2. Value Individual Contributions

The individual efforts and contribution of the employees play a vital part in the company's overall goals and direction. It is the responsibility of the leader to make the workers realize this crucial factor. When employees are aware of how their efforts create an impact on the organization, regardless of how big or small their contributions are, employees will take pride and be engaged in their work.

You do not have to reward your employees with gifts or awards every time someone performs great at a specific task. A simple *"Thank You"* or *"Great job"* will suffice at most times. These meaningful words of acknowledgment and appreciation of the effort to build loyalty and encourage employees to work even harder. In the word of human nature, nothing is more worthwhile than feeling valued.

3. A Home Away from Home

Your employees spend most of their time at work. This is their home away from home. Sometimes a lack of motivation occurs because their workplace does not have a "positive vibe" or a positive feel. Ask the workforce what they feel about their workspace and what would make them more comfortable.

Create an environment that has positive energy. Post positive quotes or motivational pictures. Make the break or lunchroom more inviting. In common places, post leadership development articles or motivational infographics. Don't forget the plants or foliage to help create a serene workplace environment. Encourage members of the team to make their workspace their own, of course in good taste.

Another best practice is to have regular potluck-style lunches; this is really a great way to grow relationships, enjoy different cultural foods, and develop a sense of team.

Employees should feel cared for and happy

Did I mention that we need our workforce to develop the organizations to develop into the best it can become? When it comes to making your employees feel cared for, most times, this is an overlooked component of leadership. One of the worst things I ever heard an employee say was, "I hate working here." Steve was a solid worker, a medium performer, the kind of employee that came in, did his job and went home. One day he was in the breakroom as I passed and heard him with an angry tone say those four powerful words. His frustration was apparent, and his words cut into me as a personal failure. As a leader, someone that guides others, if you are creating a work environment that people hate to come to, this is a reflection of your leadership and ability to influence.

Employees who feel appreciated and valued by their leaders and organization for that matter are more likely to go beyond the call of duty to serve the organization in reaching the vision. Another component to consider here is that when employees feel valued, they hold themselves accountable for their responsibilities, and this is where ownership of the company's mission blossoms. It is a simple equation: show your employees you care and value them and watch how they care and value your organization.

Helping Them Grow Personally

In the first chapter, we discussed Servant Leadership. Assisting members of your workforce to grow is a strong component of servant leadership practice. When we help them grow and get to the next level of their career, you are fueling the heater of inspiration and motivation. Let's stay on the path of the intent of this chapter; when we are keeping our workforce motivated, they are dedicated, loyal, and much easier to coach.

A significant element of helping our employees' personal development is taking an interest in their lives outside the workplace. Each one of our employees has individual tastes, motivations, beliefs, and values. This is a big component of what motivates them internally. People will walk to the ends of the earth to provide for their families and understanding their drive will allow you to coach them better when it aligns with their values and direction. One of my clients has about 125 employees, and they are constantly hiring. While writing this chapter, I was introduced to a new employee named James. During his orientation, he was scheduled for a driver training class at noon. The class was about 6 miles away from the office. James mentioned he would need to leave about 10:00 to get to the class. We explained that it was just a few miles away and he could leave about 20 minutes to 12. James mentioned that he did not have a car and would need to walk there. After a further conversation on the matter, we realized that James lived about 12 miles from the office and walked to work. We were amazed that James was on time every day until we heard this story and never mentioned his challenge.

What motivates a man to walk 12 miles, work a 10-hour day, then walk the 12 miles home? Regardless of the reasons, the desire and motivation were strong enough to make this a mission to succeed. Of course, we assisted James with getting back and forth to work until he could get a reliable mode of transportation.

Do not just expect; SET AN EXAMPLE!

When you are setting off to coach people, they often take a hard look at you and determine if they want to be guided by you. Of course, being in a position of responsibility, they should be listening to your guidance, but without respect, all you are sharing are words. This is why it is essential that you set the standards by being the best example possible. Members of your team are watching you, even when you think no one is looking. When you are developing a plan to inspire and motivate, nothing helps you more to gain respect then to be the change you want to see in them. Set the example for others to follow.

Think about it a second, as a leader, you have a strong and inspiring personality, have a position the others inspire to attain, and hopefully have a magnetism that attracts people. When you are in the trenches, doing the work, experiencing what the workforce is experiencing, this gains respect and grows your ability to influence.

Here are a few tips that can help you inspire your team members:

1. Be the Authority

You need to be a master at your job, understand your leadership practice, and have a strong reputation in your career field. Having an in-depth understanding of your industry and business grows trust and gives confidence to those following you.

2. Watch what you say

There is a Japanese proverb that says, "the reputation of a thousand years may be determined by the conduct of one hour". Sometimes in the heat of the day, we will say things with heated emotion that may not sit well with others. You always have to be aware of your surroundings, have strong self-awareness, and be a student of your emotional intelligence. Of course, if you allow your emotions to dictate your actions with words, bring an understanding to that as quickly as possible.

3. Be a good listener

Sometimes, as leaders, we are so focused on giving direction, we forget to pay attention and listen. A good rule of thumb here is that the individuals that are doing the work are the experts at the work being done. This means including them in strategy, asking their opinions, and never changing a work process without their input.

4. The Buck Stops Here

President Harry S. Truman had a wood plate on his desk that read, "The buck stops here." Back in his day, the saying, "pass the buck" basically meant passing responsibility to someone else. This actually originated in the frontier days while playing poker. Players would use a knife with a buckhorn handle to keep track of who would be next to deal the cards. If a player did not want to deal, they would pass the responsibility by passing the "buck" to the next player. President Truman's sign was a reminder that he had the overall responsibility and there would be no passing of the buck. While we are on the subject of President Truman's wood desk plate sign, just in case you ever find yourself on Jeopardy, on the reverse of the "buck stops here" plate was the phrase, "I'm from Missouri". But I digress.

Credit: Harry S. Truman Library

An old adage in leadership is to give all the credit and take all the blame. This is so very true, and in my career, both as a worker and consultant, there have been countless times supervisors and managers throw others under that proverbial bus. This is a horrible practice and one that should be stopped immediately. When you are in a position of responsibility, you are responsible for everything your workforce does or doesn't do. Nothing will demotivate a workforce more than when there is a finger pointed at the workforce.

5. Finally, Let Them Do the Work

Stop micromanaging! Communicate the mission, vision, values, and goals. Then step back and let the team innovate. Setting this example for the team will encourage others in positions of responsibility to do the same. It will also allow your team to open their wings and fly.

This chapter was all about tips to assist you in developing an inspired and motivated workforce. This has to be a crucial component to developing your highly engaged workforce. Once they are motivated and inspired, this will allow you a fertile foundation for coaching to occur.[11]

---

[11] 7 Simple Ways to Lead by Example, Retrieved From https://www.inc.com/brent-gleeson/7-ways-to-lead-by-example.html

CHAPTER 6

THE PRACTICE OF COACHING

"Without a coach, people will never reach their maximum capabilities."
-Bob Nardelli

The past five chapters have been some foundation needed to approach the next chapters. As we now start to discuss the practice of coaching, keep in mind the past few chapters and how those skills fit into your coaching model. As always, take notes and write your questions, so you are able to research them later.

The practice of coaching has been around for a very long time. Suppose you are a student of history, stories of coaching surfaces with different names and titles; teachers, mentors, elders, gurus, advisors, and Jedi Masters (sorry that got away from me there at the end). The tradition of coaching and focusing on the development of others comes under the top five competencies for leaders. Nevertheless, despite the listed importance of this crucial skill, coaching is most often overlooked or is not a competency leaders have been taught to accomplish.

When we think about being transformative in our leadership approach, the failure in the ability or opportunity to coach ties our hands behind our back; as we try to push a bicycle up a hill with a rope, nothing will happen. Our job as leaders is to get work done through other people and to get the very best out of them

This is why the practice of coaching is vital for employee, leadership, and organizational success. Coaching needs to be front and center in getting the mission completed to reach the overall vision of the company. It has to be said and shouted from the rooftops; it's high time that organizations shift their focus towards coaching all levels of their organization.

Even though this has been known for years, there are still some common reasons that leaders are not practicing this vital skill include:

The lack of 'time commitment' needed

Everything takes time, and most individuals in positions of responsibilities have their own list of tasks that must be done daily. So, when it comes to developing a plan to coach employees, this lack of time causes this oversight.

Lack of training in the practice of coaching

Leaders are expected to be the jack-of-all-trades, but at the end of the day, we must know that they are a human too. Not all leaders are born coaches. They might know how to do things, but teaching those things is a completely different side of the coin. Therefore, the lack of training in skills needed to be the best coach possible is yet another issue in executing the practice of coaching.

Consider it will slow down the workers' current progress

Often leaders choose to prioritize other important things rather than investing time in coaching their employees. They believe that if their workers focus on learning new things, they might slow down the existing production in turn. Hence, they put aside the idea of coaching. This is really a not seeing the forest for the tree's mentality.

It makes no difference what the excuses are, and individuals can come up with many. The bottom line is that in today's workforce, both leadership and organizational success need to be set on a solid foundation of coaching. You, as the leader have to learn the methodology, develop the needed skills, and **MUST** make the time to employ these methods.

As you prepare to learn the skills to coaching higher performance of your workforce, consider the following points as foundational.

Promote a culture of building awareness

It is important that you, as a leader, promote a culture of developing both situational and self-awareness. Every person present in the organization must be aware of all the things and operations taking place in the organization. Also, members of the workforce must understand how they are responsible for making the organization successful.

Give your workforce a pledge

By giving them a pledge, you will help them succeed and get to the next level. As their leader, you are responsible for helping them grow to the next level. I know that in this book already, you have read this a couple of times. Not to be overstated, but this needs to be overstated. Make a commitment to your workforce that you will be dedicated and committed to their personal and professional growth.

Create an environment of growth through coaching

After you have given your pledge, now it is paramount that you create a culture and environment where coaching is a mandatory part of individual growth.

When you are coaching employees, you are educating them with new or innovative knowledge, teaching them new skills, or helping them master the skills they already have, which will promote their growth.

When you set these three practices as rules for you and your leadership, watch how your team's growth and development thrive.

Does It Sound Easy?

To this point, coaching may sound easy, but in fact, it can be very challenging. But like anything that is challenging, the end result is also very rewarding. As we go through our coaching methodologies, we have to move from a position of teaching to being more of a facilitator, allowing the 'coachee' to see the importance of their development and the importance of them making that development happen.

Think about it, who is going to be more successful: a manager who tells or directs others on what to do or how to do it, or a leader who joins you in setting an example of how to do something in such a way that you can achieve the most successful of outcomes. Which one will be more effective? Of course, the commitment to coaching that sets these two apart.

As we push through the rest of this book, we have already laid some wet concrete in setting our coaching foundation. As these practices become hardened and become hardwired, your practice and experience with coaching others will grow.

The Practice of Coaching

Let us now look at a few crucial skills that you need to remember when setting up your coaching practice:

- Your foundational leadership style should be that of service.
- Ensure you develop a close professional rapport with the "coachee." They should know and feel that you truly care about them and their growth.
- Coaching employees takes time, and you must be willing to invest the time and be dedicated to the overall process.
- When coaching, there is nothing that is going on, which is more important than you being there with that member. Stay focused, be present, and use your active listening skills.
- Use leading questions and paraphrase as needed.
- Try to find an alternative place for coaching other than your office. Find a way, if you can, to meet them where they are or on neutral ground.

When you are committed to the exercise of coaching, you are setting the standards for others to follow you. It is all about making others a better version of themselves. When you help them succeed and get to the next level of their success, watch what that does for your leadership success, and more importantly, the success of the organization.

Before you begin your practice of coaching, add this line to your job description; *you will become a leader that is committed to giving your workforce the tools to become the next generation of leaders in the world.*

Let's take a look at how best to start your coaching practice. It begins with analyzing the person and situation even before you initiate individual conversations.

CHAPTER 7

ANALYZE FIRST TO COACH BEST

I have been looking forward to writing this chapter ever since I developed the outline. This will be something that is really important for everyone reading to recognize, as it is a persistent error that most managers make when dealing with members of the workforce.

Remember, back in chapter 4, we talked about my interaction with Jim? I watched Jim fail to meet expectations, leading to my big mistake of not giving him the benefit of the doubt, and instead of growing and coaching him, I labeled him and called him 'cancer' to the organization. I did not recognize the opportunity to analyze his need for guidance and to share my leadership, skills, and experience. He needed someone to coach him when, in reality, my behavior did not display an ounce of leadership whatsoever.

Before we get into the how-to analyze a situation to coach best, I want to take a minute to talk about switching your mental focus when it comes to labeling members of your workforce. When things do not go the way, supervisors expect them to go, finger-pointing always seems to be the norm. In my book, 'Ultimate Leadership 10 Rules for Success,' rule #3 is 'There are no problems, just solutions.' The chapter gives advice for not pointing fingers and instead of finding solutions. Along with finger-pointing, most times it is inevitable that management roles will find a culprit and slap a label on those in the workforce that was to blame.

Again, back to the story I told about Jim. What was easy for me to do after seeing his behavior was to label Jim a subpar employee, even going so far as calling him cancer to the organization. When I was in my 'horrible as leader days,' this was standard practice for me. As I went through my day, I would find myself not interacting with the employees that I disliked or had preconceived opinions about while being jovial and friendly with the employees that I liked or favored. My behavior was a textbook definition of favoritism.

Stop Labeling Employees

Everyone we come in contact with inside or outside of work has different opinions, beliefs, and values than we do. When people do not believe what we do, most people tend to label, make fun of, and consider them as lesser people. It just happens but bringing this practice into your leadership roles and practice is not very professional. This was who I was in my younger days of first being a supervisor. I made this horrible behavior a part of my leadership style.

Ladies and gentlemen, this practice has to stop, and we have to get on the side of treating every single employee with the same focus, respect, and commitment to achieving next-level growth. As soon as you treat someone differently, you are compromising your leadership integrity. As leaders, it is your responsibility to get the very best out of the workforce. Not to get the very best out of half the crew or your favored workforce members, but each and every employee working under our management.

It is why, as a matter of practice, we have to be fair, consistent, and nonbiased in all our day-to-day responsibilities, and that begins with putting a stop to labeling employees.

The Law of the Excluded Middle

There is a logical principle called the *'Law of the Excluded Middle.'* In short, as stated by Aristotle, *"there cannot be an intermediate between contraindications, but of one subject we must either affirm or deny any one predicate."* What that means is when we label employees as cancer, losers, horrible employees, the law of the excluded middle tells us that those employees either are or aren't that label. There is no in-between, and if we believe those employees are cancers, we are less likely to invest in their professional development. When leaders label, we are now creating an unfair advantage for those members of the workforce. When you are in a position of responsibility, you have to ensure everyone is treated with the utmost respect and gets your very best of attention.

What does all of this have to do with analyzing people and situations before coaching? This is the first step in ensuring that any preconceived biases or unfairness do not influence your judgment. It allows you a clear and open mind giving you the opportunity to attain all the facts before setting off on the path you need to take. This is an extremely crucial foundation to the success of coaching.

Analyzing the Need for Coaching

Let's begin with the best practice of dealing with performance issues. Your first step is to determine what is influencing their performance. Operational issues can be placed in one of four categories:

1. **Training** - There is a disconnect from when the employee went through initial training not retaining the needed material, an issue with how they were trained, and if components of the training process were not completed correctly. This is why developing instructional competencies are important when training a new employee. This way, once the training is

completed, both the trainee and trainer can sign the task was taught, and the proper level of competency has been met. One of the number one excuses when meeting with an employee about a performance issue is, *"no one ever taught me that,"* this is why documenting training is essential.

2. **Environment** – It could be that something in the employee's environment is causing the performance issue. It could be weather, noise, or even peers, literally anything that is not making their environment conducive enough to attain high performance.

3. **Equipment** – A greater challenge with performance issues is the equipment they are using to do their job. It makes a significant difference if the equipment is old or broken. Ensuring the employees have the best equipment to do their jobs is essential to ensure high job performance and productivity.

4. **Behavior** – Sometimes, it is just the employee having a behavioral challenge, and it is up to the supervisor to get to the bottom of the issue. In the workplace, employees want to be treated with respect, as peers, and as adults. If there are behavioral issues, there must be a catalyst, and when we get to the issue, we can hopefully improve their performance.

When you first identify a performance issue, this does not mean you have to jump straight to a coaching session, whereas, on the other hand, if you were using progressive discipline, it may warrant a verbal or written. Take your time to determine the best way to approach the particular employee.

5 Steps Process

Now you know there is a possible issue, and you have to determine if the issue has merit or not. Use this five-step process to gather the needed information:

1. **Observe**

    Observe performance and gather information about what you are suspecting. Sometimes individuals may come and cue you in on an issue. As a rule of thumb, use the trust but verify method, do not take their word for it, do your own observation, and see if the complaint/issue holds water.

2. **Communicate**

    After you have observed your team member, have a chat with the employee and share what you have noticed. Ask them if they are having or noticing any issues with their performance or how they are performing their duties.

    If there are issues that are identified, then work together to develop a solution. Make the determination together if the employee feels they can correct their performance. This can be a stand-up meeting and nothing in a formal setting. In the next couple of weeks, make sure you follow up with the employee regularly to assess their level of comfort with the change.

3. **Sit-Down Discussion**

    Occasionally there has to be more formal discussion issues that are more serious or follow-up discussions to the first one where no improvement was noticed. This should be a more formal sit-down discussion. This conversation is still based on facilitation, and you are not giving the answers or finding a solution. You state the importance of meeting expectations, overview what was discussed in the past, and the expected resolution. Then ask the employee to give you a specific commitment as to how the performance issue will improve. This is your chance to provide assistance and let the employee know that you are there for them and ready to help in any way. Follow up with the employee a few times a week for the next two weeks and inspire them as needed.

4. Coaching Analysis

Time for the coaching analysis. I have been using this coaching analysis for over a decade now, and it truly gives me guidance as to how you can handle issues with employees[12]. This was something I came across, and I wanted to share it with you as well. Make this part of your coaching toolbox.

Coaching Analysis: What is influencing unsatisfactory performance?		
Identify behavior discrepancy. ⬇		
Is it worth your time and effort?	➡ NO	Don't waste your time on it.
⬇ YES		
Do they know performance is unsatisfactory?	➡ NO	Give them feedback.
⬇ YES		
Do they know what they're supposed to do?	➡ NO	Tell them.
⬇ YES		
Do they know how to do it?	➡ NO	Train them or give them practice.
⬇ YES		
Do they know why they should do it?	➡ NO	Tell them.
⬇ YES		
Are there obstacles beyond their control?	➡ YES	Remove obstacles.
⬇ NO		
Do they think your way will not work?	➡ YES	Convince them.
⬇ NO		
Do they think their way is better?	➡ YES	Convince them.
⬇ NO		
Do they think something else is more important?	➡ YES	Explain priorities.
⬇ NO		
Are there positive consequences to them for performing appropriately?	➡ NO	Give positive reinforcement.
⬇ YES		
Are there negative consequences to them for performing appropriately?	➡ YES	Remove negative consequences or balance with positive consequences.
⬇ NO		
Do they anticipate future negative consequences for performing appropriately?	➡ YES	Correct their understanding.
⬇ NO		
Are there positive consequences to them for performing inappropriately?	➡ YES	Change consequences.
⬇ NO		
Are they performing inappropriately without receiving negative consequences?	➡ YES	Deliver negative consequences.
⬇ NO		
Are personal problems interfering?	➡ YES	Accommodate the problem or get employee to solve your problem.
⬇ NO		
Could they do it if they choose to do it?	➡ NO	Transfer, demote, or terminate.
⬇ NO		
Use the coaching discussion to change their behavior choices.	➡	

Figure 7-1

---

[12] link of the Image that's attached above https://hr.williams.edu/files/2014/05/Coaching-Analysis_Handout.pdf

5. Write Down Everything

When you have a discussion with employees, remember the best practice of documenting the conversation. This is your personal record of what took place, what was discussed, and when it happened. Remember, this is a facilitated discussion, and you should both sign the performance improvement plan (PIP). A PIP can be as simple as having the following sections:

- Employees Name – Who the PIP is for.
- Areas Needing Improvement – This can be outlined as an area of responsibility, such as data entry or resource management.
- Performance Challenges – This is the outline of what was found during the observation phase.
- Plan for Improvement – Ask the employee to develop the plan that needs to be completed to polish their performance.
- Timeframe for Improvement – This should be a time both you and the employee agree is a focused time to change the performance.
- Failure to Meeting PIP – This should be an accountability for not meeting expectations of the PIP. This could be something like retraining, transfer to another set of responsibilities, or ending your professional relationship. The latter should occur only after adequate retraining and support.
- Signed/Dated by Coach and Employee.
- There is a sample PIP in Chapter 4

Coaching the Face-to-Face Discussion

Before holding your coaching discussion, you needed to have completed the coaching analysis form (figure 7-1) . The coaching analysis will guide you on whether or not this is the right next step to conduct. You are trying to change a performance issue or create a different behavior.

- Hold the coaching in a private area. You do not want anyone in earshot of this personal discussion.
- Start the discussion by getting right to the heart of the matter. Say something like, *"Paul, you have not been following the correct process, and you are backing up shipping with your performance."* Be very specific. Paul must admit there is a performance problem.
- Ask Paul for some solutions in how this issue can be corrected. Facilitate ideas, but Paul must come up with his own solutions. Share your thoughts on correcting the issue in a pinch, but this should be a last resort.
- Once a solution has been agreed upon, ensure that there is a mutual agreement on what action needs to be taken to resolve the issue and when it will occur. Of course, it should happen immediately.
- One of the most important steps to any coaching discussion is the follow up with any constructive or corrective feedback. As soon as you notice Paul making an effort to correct the problem, give positive feedback to help reinforce the change.

Sometimes Coaching Fails

I brought this up before. It needs to be repeated. Sometimes, an individual is not cut out for your organization, and you may have to end your professional relationship. Just ensure that you have given the employee a fair shot at making it work.

Coaching is a great recipe for success. Using the coaching analysis is a great way to prepare yourself for having a productive coaching discussion. Now, let's look at coaching individuals with low self-confidence or low self-esteem.

CHAPTER 8

COACHING LOW SELF CONFIDENCE AND LOW SELF ESTEEM

One of the biggest challenges you will run across when coaching others is dealing with individuals that have low self-confidence and low self-esteem. Once you explore the practice of coaching your workforce and truly get to know what people think and believe about themselves, you will be amazed to see how many people in the workforce suffer from these two afflictions.

Low Self Confidence

Self-confidence outlines the feelings related to competence, ability, and expertise the employee believes in themselves to accomplish anything. When you have a high degree of self-confidence, you are aware of your strengths, work on your weaknesses, and have a positive view of who you are. When you have low self-confidence, you may feel self-doubt, be withdrawn or compliant with others. Another challenge is those with low self-confidence have a tendency not to trust others. With that being said, there is a degree of individuals with low self-confidence who feel confident in their leader's relationship, yet still believes they are not skillful in doing their job. This is why developing a rapport and a trusting relationship is crucial to employee development. Once you can identify this, it creates a great foundation for helping these folks become more trusting in their overall ability.

Low Self Esteem

Self Esteem, in a nutshell, is what individuals believe about who they are as people. Most of the time, people will have a fake sense of belief around other people, but deep inside, they are not comfortable in their own skin. Low self-esteem can also have a huge impact on creating low self-confidence and poor self-respect. When identifying individuals with a self-esteem issue, professionals in the psychology world do not like using the terms high and low to categorize self-esteem. Instead, they use terms like healthy, beneficial for high and reduced, decreased, or impaired for low self-esteem.

People with a high degree of self-esteem can seem conceited, self-absorbed, or narcissistic. This type of behavior is not beneficial and hence noted as impaired or reduced. In my experience, people that are conceited, who believe they are great, actually are hiding the fact that they do not like themselves, and when I say in my experience, this was me. I was so self-absorbed and conceited in my younger immature days that I hid the fact I did not know everything like I thought I did.

In the workforce, it is important you peel away the layers of the onion to get deeper into the understanding of those you are trying to coach. This only happens when members of your workforce know, like, and trust you. If you do not have a friendly professional relationship with them, they cannot drop their guard or defenses to share their fears and concerns. Yet, when you can connect with people and truly listen to them talk, you get a sense of who they are and where their motivation rests. As you try to pull the best out of them, this will illuminate low self-confidence and reduced low self-esteem.

Let's take a look at the coaching process separately for low self-confidence and reduced self-esteem.

Coaching People with Low Self Confidence

Before you think that your employee has low self-confidence, do your homework and investigate this possibility. Does the employee seek constant reassurance? Does their insecurity or lack of engagement have a negative impact on team dynamics? Are they sabotaging their career because they are insecure about their abilities? I am sure there are many more questions you can ask. Just remember, when you are focusing on the employee and taking an active interest in coaching them, you will begin to see them in a whole different light.

- Help them see the challenge and have them admit it truly exists – This is easier said than done. Again, the secret is that you have to have a great rapport, and the employee must know, like, and trust you - let's also add respect to that list.
- Be honest with the employee about what you have been noticing – We, of course, are not psychologists. We can only report what we see. We are not trying to find out the catalyst of their low confidence, heck that can go back to childhood; we can only move forward from what we are seeing now. Share with them what you see or what you have noticed. Maybe in meetings, they become defensive when challenged; perhaps they do not feel comfortable speaking up. Whatever the situation, be as specific as possible.

When talking with an employee about their challenges, remember, this may be a very stressful experience for the employee and could cause some anxiety. Sometimes, as leaders, we see the greatness in someone before they see the greatness in themselves.

With one such employee, we will call her Betty, I saw greatness in her and had a great plan to get her to her next level of success. She had a high degree of self-confidence, almost to a fault. A bit of background, Betty was a paramedic. She was strong clinically and delivered great patient care. I wanted her to take more of a leadership role as she was well liked by the workforce.

As time went by, she began accepting more and more responsibility. Betty even took the lead on a couple of big projects. Then I began noticing that Betty started to withdraw from the team; she was not speaking up in meetings. In one instance, we chatted before the meeting about how to bring a topic forward, yet she failed to bring up the topic. When stronger leaders challenged her during meetings, she would change her opinion and give in to the team's wishes. So, it was time to work on her self-confidence.

I set up a meeting with Betty, laid out my opinions, and basically laid out in front of her what I thought about her performance and why I came to the conclusions I did. As the conversation went deeper and deeper, I realized Betty began wringing her hands, then she began rocking back and forth, and I noticed her breathing was increasing and getting deeper.

I remember thinking, *"Is she having an anxiety attack?"* Well, yes, she was. I had scratched away at her defense and was calling out her weakness which she was not a fan of. I shared this story here to ensure that when you are talking with employees about their weaknesses, they may not be as happy as you are that you found their kryptonite.

1. **Manage expectations** – This is something that you should do together. When you are coaching people about their self-confidence, get them to agree to take one little step at a time. With Betty, I told her if she did not agree with the team that I would support her in her difference of opinion. Her role was that she just needed to speak up and share her views.

2. **Give good positive feedback** – You have to be the one to grow the areas they feel confident. Get them to learn about their strengths, give a pat on their back, have peers ask them for help. Back to Betty, one of the ways I helped her build her confidence, she was firm in her ability to take care of patients with cardiac issues. So, Betty became the Subject Matter Expert in Cardiology and dealing with cardiac issues. When people would have any sort of cardiac questions, they went to Betty. When someone needed remediation, they went to Betty. Little by little, she grew in her skills and became strong in her confidence.

Low self-confidence is an Achilles heel for a lot of people out there. It is up to you are their coach to assist them in stepping outside their comfort zone and grow into the greatness you see in them.

Coaching Self Esteem

Self-esteem is the feeling of self-worth. Like reduced self-confidence, workers often question their decisions and capabilities. Here are some tips that you can use when coaching someone who has reduced self-worth.

1. **Put them in a position where they have to make more decisions** – When you empower people, they feel good about that responsibility, then in turn better about themselves. This does not have to be big decisions, just something that is in their realm of expertise. I remember giving Betty the lead in helping the organization pick our next cardiac monitor. I laid out the expectations, gave her my opinion about how to get this process done, and she ran the field research as to which monitor would make the very best tool.
2. **Get them to trust their feelings** – It is that 6th sense. Most of the time, our instincts are right, while other times, they smack

us right in the face. Yet, we still trusted them. Sometimes we are right other times, we are wrong, but mistakes + reflection = wisdom. When helping someone overcome confidence and esteem issues, you have to equip them to handle mistakes. That is one of the reasons they have issues in the first place; they do not want to fail and be made fun of. If we do not help them develop the skills that will help them in this time of need, they will always be fearful of being more confident or trusting themselves.

3. **In business, it is always about supporting the team** – But you do not have to please everyone all the time. Teach them that it is okay not to base decisions on what everyone else may want or be thinking. People have the right to disagree; this is what we want folks to tell us their opinions and consider different options. Along with this is the ability to say no when you have no more capacity to take on more work. This is one of my teaching moments with people; when I know, they will not say no, I give them more and more to do. Eventually, the lesson comes to the surface. You say no to the project and not the person.

4. **Think positive thoughts** – Teach them the importance of retraining their subconscious mind. That negative self-talk is never our friend, yet it is only saying what we have programmed it to tell us. By coaching the employee to challenge the negative with positive is a great way to get them to start believing in themselves.

5. **Help them develop a vision for their future** – We are in the business of developing our organizations to the next level. We do that by growing our workforce to the next level. Help them develop a vision, create goals to reach the vision, and then plans to reach the goals. Then walk with them on the journey of reaching their vision.

The Gibbs Reflective Cycle

I want to touch on one more tool to help with developing self-confidence and self-esteem. It is called the Gibbs Reflective Cycle. Developed by Professor Graham Gibbs, it was outlined in his book "Learning by Doing." This process is beneficial to individuals learn from situations, especially when they may not go as planned.

This really helps individuals think about the 'why' they feel the way they do. When I coach people with low confidence or reduced esteem, I teach them this process and ask them to spend some alone time going through the stages in a particular topic.

Gibbs Reflective Cycle

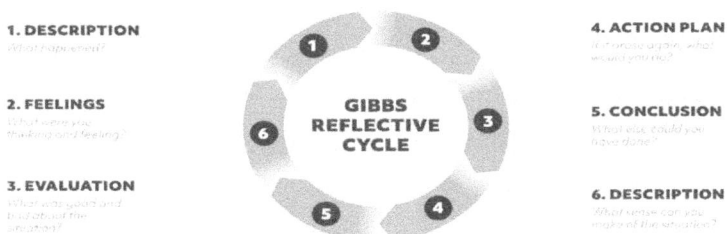

1. **Description** – This is where you set the stage by determining what happened when it occurred, who was there, what was done, and what was the outcome. This is the foundation for everything else to grow from.
2. **Feelings** – Reflect on the feelings and thoughts you had about the experience. Ask yourself, what feelings did you have at the time this happened? How did this affect your thinking at the time? How do you feel about this event afterward and today? The beliefs that you take from this will cause you to carry a weight that may affect future events.

3. **Evaluation** – Focus on the positive and negative things that occurred at the time. Think about what was good and bad about the experience or event. What led to the positives and negatives? The realization is that everyone makes mistakes and fails. It is how you determine the why that is important. What's the equation? Oh yes, Mistakes + Reflection = Wisdom.

4. **Analysis** – This is an essential step in this cycle. This is where you try to make sense of what happened and try to develop an understanding of the event. This is the reflection as to what could have been done differently or better. Ask yourself to explain what happened, what caused things to go bad or well? How did you respond? How could you have responded differently?

5. **Conclusion** – In this cycle, you can choose two different conclusions: a general or a specific conclusion. General is transferable, while specific is focused on your personal situation. The questions for your consideration, what have I learned? Think generally and specifically. What is it you can do better now? What could you have done differently? What tools or skills do you need to develop to handle this better?

6. **Action Plans** – This is the secret sauce of any reflection; you have to know what you will need to do in the future to improve next time. It is all about being able to adapt actions and improve skills. How will you react differently in the same situation? Think about how and where you can use your knowledge and experiences.

Somewhere along the path of life, we all have had to deal with low self-confidence and self-esteem. If a coach out there could have helped us navigate the waters, life could have been much easier. Well, here you are you have a worker that may need your skills to guide them through the murky waters and help them build themselves up. Once we help them grow, they are able to help our organization grow. That's how important the role of coaching truly is.

CHAPTER 9

COACHING HIGH PERFORMING EMPLOYEES

Believe it or not, coaching high-performing employees is not as easy as it sounds. These are the employees who are setting the standards for others to follow. They have developed a long list of achievements by prioritizing their needs, envisioning new possibilities, taking on new responsibilities, and feeling accountable for what they do. In fact, they are always open to take on new challenges.

These highly motivated members of the workforce follow the 80/20 rule work, which is to prioritize the 20% of the factors to produce the best possible results. They have a gift of identifying and recognizing the best possible factors, elements, or assets and use them efficiently to create maximum value. They demonstrate a mindset to learn new skills and sharpen the old ones, and make their leaders say, "I wish I had 10 more just like you." As amazing as it is to lead high-performing and motivated employees, there is also a downside.

They are always driven toward the next achievement, as they are never genuinely satisfied with their performance. They constantly strive for perfection and are often incredibly hard on themselves. It may seem that guiding high-performing employees should be easier, but it can more complicated. Moreover, they can easily become disengaged if they don't receive enough coaching and mentoring from their supervisors. When high-performing employees are pushed to learn and develop work skills, they become more equipped to do their job well. Likewise, when they are coached on their performance, they get motivated to go the extra mile to produce high-quality results.

Being a high-performing employee myself, it was essential for me to self-reflect and view who I am and what I wanted to become. The realization came about 15 years ago as I was going through my professional career. I was doing everything I could to make a name for myself and grow my professional reputation. My goal was to become overly exposed nationally within my career field. On the home front, my department was managing all the clinical and medical aspects of a High-Performance Emergency Medical Services (EMS) Organization in Fort Worth, Texas, called MedStar.

This was a premier Emergency Medical Services organization, and I held the top clinical position next to the Medical Director of the organization. At the time, this was my dream job. My department was made up of high performers (which was what I expected under my direction and leadership). We produced high-quality results and skill development programs to ensure that the citizens of Fort Worth received the highest quality of care from our amazing Emergency Medical Technicians and Paramedics.

MedStar was responding to about 100k requests for service in a year and had about 350 employees. We also had 40 or more so ambulances on the street at any given time. I was focused and committed to ensuring that my department ran with efficiency, effectiveness, and professionalism.

As I developed within my career, I was recognized nationally in my career field and was a sought-after speaker in my industry. I was honored to be part of a professional association, such as the Board of Directors. The achievements just kept racking up. In

2008 I was under contract with a major healthcare publisher, who commissioned my friend Rosie Adam and me to write a 'Critical Care' textbook. It seemed that my career was on a trajectory that would allow me to achieve ultimate success. I mean, this is what having a successful career is all about, right? I was living my life by the statement, *"He who dies with the most toys wins."* Of course, for me, the toys that I wanted to achieve in life were professional accolades. I wanted the titles, bigger positions, and to make as much money as possible.

Then one day, my Vice President made an offhand comment about me that caused me to sit back and re-evaluate my approach to how I was managing my career. This was a very simple comment that had an enormous influence over me.

He said, *"Chris, you are the most driven individual I have ever met."*

I remember thinking that it was a good thing to say about me and felt an immediate sense of pride in my accomplishments. However, in the same conversation, he continued, *"Sometimes, weaknesses can be overproduced strengths."*

It took me a few days to make sense of these two statements, as they played on a continuous loop in my head over and over again. I was really harping on what was said to me. I was beginning to believe that the comments made were not meant as a compliment. Instead, they were a wake-up call.

Was I missing something in his comment, was there a hidden message or agenda for me?

Just for the record, this VP, who caused me to reflect upon myself, is a good man and powerful leader. I considered him to be a mentor and friend to this day. In our later conversation, he told me about the hidden message in his comment: "it was okay to be driven but think about the people who help you in your career as you progress. It would help if you remembered that you are growing because of them, not despite them".

So, in retrospect, I considered myself a high performer. However, I might not have been the best resource for my peers and the workforce. As I was working full steam ahead, kicking up a wake of accomplishments, padding my resume, and reaching for the stars, it never occurred to me that I was drowning those who were trying to walk with me.

Coaching High Performers

Even though high-performing employees are 'go-getters'; they are far from being left alone on the coaching scale. They set the standards for others to follow and get work done perfectly. However, they often miss out on other intangible elements. In fact, they may need just as much coaching as a low performer. I know that it might sound surprising to hear this, so let me lay out my thoughts for you. During your career, you will come across people who are on the verge of becoming high performers and those who have potential but are not living up to it for whatever reason. Therefore, it is crucial to know where they lay before you begin to coach them.

When you look at a particular individual, you will need to coach them according to their scale of performance and potential.

1. High Performance/Low Potential
2. High Performance/High Potential
3. Low Performance/Low Potential
4. Low Performance/High Potential

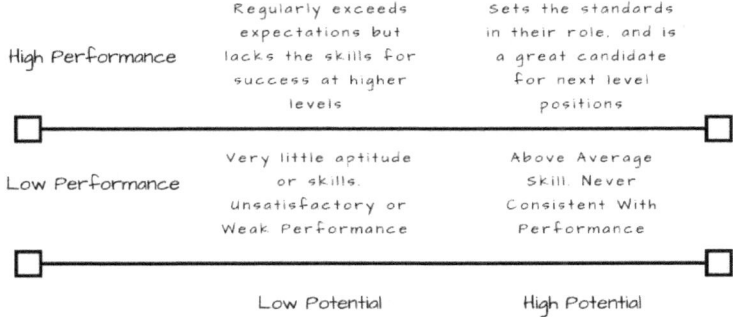

This scale will give you a great head start of developing the best coaching plan.

Examine their Motivation

It is imperative to get to the foundation of what makes a high performer tick. They still have weaknesses and fears and need to overcome them to proceed to the next level. When you carry out a foundational discussion with a high performer, consider using the following approach:
- Do in-depth research into who they are?
- What are their values and beliefs?
- Determine what motivates them?
- Where does their motivational drive come from?
- Find out how they deal with their mistakes or failures?
- Determine their adaptability to new situations, circumstances, pressures, environment, culture, or people.

One of the things I have found in my career of coaching high performers is that many of them have hidden secrets. Some high performers do what they do best because they have a controlling nature. The best way to control what happens around them is to create an environment that they want to be in. Think about it; we always stay out of the way of those who are setting the standards most of the time. Even though they are being productive, you must coach them so that they can release the feeling of wanting to be in control.

If a person likes to be in control, this could lead to a problem with change. Change is unavoidable in most organizations. When it becomes necessary to change a high performer's process, change becomes a hard pill to swallow for them. If control is a characteristic trait, change does not go down as easily as you would like to think.

Can high performers be "the most driven people you have ever met in your life?" This was a considerable eye-opening statement that changed my approach to my career positioning and responsibilities. It is great to be ambitious, but it should never be built on the backs of the people you are responsible for, or should I say responsible to.

Be aware of the halo effect, which is when the boss sees past the known flaws because of their high-performers independence.

Coaching a High Performer

There are some great coaches out there, and they have developed some great tools for us to use. Not that I have a reason to reinvent the wheel. One of the world's most popular high-performance coaches is Rich Litvin. He created the 'Exponential Coaching Model,' which outlines five strategic elements that will help you coach high performers to the next level and beyond.

1. **Deep Listening** – Be present in the session and allow yourself to become a part of the inner world of your performer. Bring out their thoughts, feelings, fears, and allow them to get to understand their feelings. Most of the time, there can be touchy topics to discuss. For high-performance coaching, it is necessary to discuss the vital areas where high performers can feel invulnerable to allow themselves to open up.

2. **Eliciting** – It is all about the vision, goals, and direction that the performer wants to go. Sometimes, they do not even know where the direction is or where it leads to. You must lay out a foundation to allow this concept to take shape and make it easier for the performer to understand.
3. **10X** – I love this element as it can guide high performers to see their achievements bigger than they have ever seen before. Use motivational methods of speaking and coaching. Guide them to have a feeling of excitement and inspire them to attain what may not have been considered before.
4. **Leadership** – This element is really for the coach. You will need to lead the performer from a place of love, respect, and deep connection. You should help them show transparency through their experiences, failures, mistakes, and learned lessons. This allows the performer to see that you are authentic, and you want to help them develop their skills.
5. **Strategy** – This element goes beyond just dealing with tasks. This is really about assisting the high performer set up an internal strategy that will help them become successful. This is about teaching them how to experience joy and satisfaction along their journey to the next level and beyond.

As you develop your skills to become the best coach possible for high performers, seek out other leaders who are in the field to learn from them. The Exponential Coaching Model is great for your toolbox. I would also recommend following Rich and learning more about his style as you develop your own.

When it comes to high performers, it is essential to treat them like any other employee. They like constructive feedback, which is meaningful to them, like being asked for opinions and assistance in developing solutions.

Coaching high performers can also lead to performance improvement in a specific skill set area, like dealing with pressure, adapting to a new environment or a new authority, resolving conflicts among team members, or working smartly. Their goals may change over time, but their objective always remains the same. Coaching high performers may also help them to develop perspective and insight to understand through intrinsic observations and become more aware of their situations and experiences.

Characteristics of High Performers

As their performance improves, they take ownership of their actions and become more responsible. For instance, if a task doesn't get completed, they take ownership of it themselves instead of blaming it on others. Organizations and coaches must learn that these individuals are unique. Moreover, they have a better understanding of how to achieve their goals along with the organizational goals. Their characteristics may include:

- Being able to achieve goals or results either individually or by working in teams.
- Assisting their managers or supervisors with team building and trust development.
- Helping their team achieve clarity in their thinking and committing to their tasks and responsibilities.
- Challenging themselves to achieve progress and success.
- Helping the team by becoming a source of support or help instead of being a threat to them.
- Identifying and solving problems the smart way.
- Being able to make insightful decisions to implement changes and overcoming barriers or obstacles as they come along.
- Having the foresight to predict what's next and then planning for the future to either take advantage of new opportunities or take precautions from the coming threats or dangers.

Coaching High Performing Employees

While coaching high performers, it is necessary to have specific objectives for them about their performance and the development of new skills. It may take place on a one-to-one basis with the performer, which can be both professional and personal. There, the coach may plan out a program with certain activities or tasks, which would be completed by the performer and then compliment them for their performance. This way, the coach may also learn how these performers may react to their accomplishments and performance, either by intrinsic or extrinsic motivation factors.

Coaching usually takes place independently of managers and supervisors. It is about being more open toward performers and establishing honest relationships. Also, it is not based on some specific feedback or training exercises. It can be done to bring in a new approach or a particular skill.

However, it does not relate to teaching, instructing, or telling the performers what to do when faced with an adverse situation where they do not know how to perform. Coaching high performers would promote greater levels of and would help them make better-informed decisions. It results in improving problem-solving skills and establishes enhanced business intelligence. Consequently, your high performers may then find out the best solutions for their usual work-related problems.

CHAPTER 10

TRANSITIONING COACHING TO MENTORSHIP

Coaching outlines the training method, where a more experienced or tenured individual assists, advises, and guides others to develop skill, knowledge, and performance. This is the crux of what we have been talking about this whole book. What are the skills and approaches for growing the members of your workforce?

At some point, individuals with who you have developed a rapport, assisted in their growth and development will leave your employment and take a new position. Heck! Of course, we want our high-performing employees to stay, primarily after we have heavily invested in their growth and development.

Yet, instead of reacting to their departure with disappointment, we should be proud of our efforts and of that individual as they take on an opportunity that boosts them to their next level. What may happen next is you find yourself in a position where those once coached will wish to continue receiving your guidance. You have now become a mentor instead of a coach. As a mentor, your role is to support, encourage, and guide people to manage their own learning, growth, and development to achieve maximum results in their career journey.

As I was writing this chapter, I received a call from a past supervisor of mine. We will call her Abby. Abby is now a director, and her role made her responsible for multiple departments and employees. Abby was a member of my leadership team functioning as a supervisor. Initially, Abby had a challenge with low self-confidence in her ability.

She also had a self-esteem issue and a wee bit of a problem with meeting deadlines. Over our time working together, we worked hard on overcoming her challenges and set goals for her development. Over the next five years, Abby grew, advanced her leadership skills, and became a beacon of influence for all who came in contact with her.

As I moved on to my next position, Abby was a bit concerned and worried. She thought her career would stall, and she wouldn't achieve the next level of her career success. At that time, I made one simple statement to Abby, "Call me any time." This was the phone call I received. The voice on the other end of the phone expressed, "Let me run something by you." It was Abby wanting to seek council on an issue she was responsible for. These types of calls happened countless times as my relationship developed from being a coach to a mentor.

This is an ultimate honor that those you guided are still seeking your assistance years after, even though you no longer work together with them. I even have a list of people in my network that were significant role models and coaches that now I consider mentors, but more importantly, they are friends.

The Mentorship Mindset

There are two types of support that I am happy to assist people with. They are Business Mentorship and Growth Mentorship. Business mentorship is when you work within the same organization, and you are in a senior position, and you can guide someone.

This person is usually someone different than your immediate supervisor or manager. Growth mentorship takes on the role when you are outside the individual's organization, and people are looking for you to share your wisdom to 'run something by you.' The relationship I have today with Abby is a growth mentorship relationship. Regardless of which type of mentoring relationship you are working with, you have to give it the very best you have in yourself. As a leader, your goal should be to create more leaders, and mentorship is the best way to do this. This is also a great way to develop your legacy, but that is a topic for another book.

Becoming the Ultimate Mentor

I have a saying throughout this book: "Sometimes, you see the greatness in people, even before they see it in themselves. As a mentor, you have to assist them in seeing that person too." When you follow these tips, it will create a solid blueprint for your mentorship success.

Be genuine and authentic – You must take a genuine interest in the person you are guiding. Being in a mentor/mentee relationship is personal and giving the type of advice that will grow someone to their next level takes an emotional connection. Be your authentic self and be accountable for the responsibility mentorships come with.

Don't Just Give Advice – Part of being a great mentor is knowing the right time to give advice. Going back to the call with Abby: After she laid out the reason for her call and what she was up against, she asked me, "So, what do you do?" My response started with a sigh and said, "That sounds like an interesting dilemma. How are you going to handle that?" Abby went on and started using her critical thinking skills.

As our discussion went on, Abby had good foresight, conceptualization, and had a tremendous go-forward plan. Before she hung up the phone with me, she thanked me for my advice and told me she could always count on me. However, I gave her no advice or shared any wisdom with her. Instead, I asked her some questions that gave her the opportunity to develop both positive and negative evidence and allowed her to develop a solution and go forward plan by herself. Sometimes, you have to allow the process just to happen.

Be Open-Minded – Always remember this is not about you; it is about the person you are helping. I can remember earlier in my career. People would come to me and ask for my advice. I would spend time thinking and creating an excellent plan for them; however, they would never use it. They would take my advice and ball it up and throw it away in the wastebasket. I remember feeling angry about this. Now, I will paraphrase my friend and mentor, John Maxwell. In one of his teachings to me, he said, "When you give advice and wisdom, that does not mean they are obliged to follow it. It is their job to take that advice, reflect on it, polish it, and make it their own. When they pass on the advice you gave them, it will look totally different." After that, keeping an open mind was a significant resource to my success at mentoring others.

Never Assume – Remember the old joke? When you ASSUME, you make an ASS out of U and ME. This also holds in a mentor/mentee relationship. Always ask for clarification, ask open-ended questions, and dig deeper. By doing so, you will be better positioned to be helpful, give feedback, or share relevant experiences.

Mistakes, Failures, Lessons Learned – This is your chance to be forthcoming about your mistakes, failures, and lessons learned. Here comes my equation again, Mistakes/Failures + Reflection = Wisdom. When you are a mentor, you break this equation down in step-by-step chunks as to how you exactly gained the wisdom you are sharing. This helps your mentee develop next-level critical thinking and problem-solving skills. More importantly, it also helps build trust and encourages the mentee to share their own mistakes and failures with you.

Be Challenging – My favorite part of being a coach and mentor is to be challenging. This allows me to push people and help identify fears and hurdles and force them to disintegrate their comfort zones and venture outside.

Your role as a mentor is to bring them to the next level of success. To do that, you have to ensure the mentee sees the greatness that abodes within them. You also need to help them set stretch goals, lean on them to make them feel uncomfortable, get them used to being uncomfortable, and avoid being fearful of taking big steps. Then slowly work them up to overcome the fear and ultimately help them reach that goal. Be their safety net, they have to walk that high wire, but you are their safety net.

Let me ask you, what is the one goal you want to achieve that just scares the heck out of you? Come on, share with the group; everyone has that one goal that they wish to achieve and have a wee bit of fear to begin. This is the value of having an experienced mentor and being in a mentor/mentee relationship is that together, goals are being accomplished. If you have that one goal that scares the heck out of you, find someone that has achieved it, and see if they will share their expertise with you.

Strategy vs. Tactics – Part of being a great mentor is teaching the strategies that someone needs to be successful. A strategy is the plan of action you use to get the desired action completed. When you set a vision, you now need to develop the goals to make that vision a reality. Goals now become the strategy for achieving the vision you have in your mind.

The missing component is teaching tactics. Most of the time, you will run across speed bumps, hurdles, and something you did not anticipate beforehand in the pursuit of your goals. It often derails an individual in the journey to reaching the vision. When you teach tactics, the mentee can understand what is happening and how to maneuver to overcome the challenge. A strategy is crucial, and tactics are vital for achieving ultimate success.

Set Expectations and Accountability - One of the first questions I like to ask people I coach, and mentor is how do you like being held accountable? It is my role to be the accountability partner for growth and development. Once the mentee sets the expectations, it is your role to hold them accountable for meeting their expectations and plans.

Remember this, nothing will stop me from working with someone quicker than their lack of accountability. Of course, you will try different ways to get them to stick to their goals. Eventually, you may come to the reality your mentee may not be ready to take their career to the next level. Consider if mentorship is right at this time.

Trust and Respect – There is no greater honor than someone wanting you to be their mentor. With that said, your goal is to add value to your mentee every time you have an interaction. It only happens when you have developed a relationship based on trust and respect. Part of this relationship is your ability to open doors for your mentee based on opportunities. Your mentee must know if you open doors for them, that is your professional integrity on the line. Developing a trusting relationship is the only way this happens.

Always Celebrate Achievements – This is an essential trait of being a mentor. When a milestone is achieved, celebrate it. You have to ensure that you are teaching your mentee the opportunity to enjoy the win. This is often a process that is overlooked as people jump from goal to goal without enjoying the spoils of the journey.

Being a mentor is an enjoyable and mutually beneficial opportunity. My growth and development have grown exponentially in the relationships developed by helping people reach their own vision and goals. Whether that comes from my teachings or the mentees teaching me a thing or two. In my opinion, there is no better professional development resource than the mentor-mentee relationship.

Conclusion

If I had my way, we would all be focused on fostering a culture of coaching in our portions of the world. I have to say that I love the art and science of leadership. I have been saying for years that you have to know and understand the science before you can paint the portrait of organizational success.

The same is true with coaching and mentoring others. This is a responsibility that cannot be overlooked and has to be met with your dedication, commitment, and responsibility to others. You have to be able to feel the passion that coaching needs to allow this in your charge to succeed.

In this book, I wanted to lay out the foundation of what you needed to know to begin a journey of coaching others. It all starts with the desire to serve others. There are people out there that need you. They may not know your name or who you are, but they hope someone will come along and help them reach their next level of success.

It is your duty to learn the skills needed to guide, coach, and develop these people. Once you develop the needed knowledge, skills, and expertise, you are now ready to take your coaching on the road and charge for your services. A piece of advice here, do not rush this process. Give yourself the gift of learning, growing, and polishing the skills necessary to be the kind of coach others deserve.

I hope this book inspired and motivated you, and if so, I'd like to ask for a favor. Please consider writing me a review on Amazon. My goal with this book is to help as many people develop the foundational skills that will help them to grow others. Your review will give this project the power for others to see the value.

Cheers to you all and good luck in your coaching careers. Please let me know how best to be a resource to you and your success.

Chris Cebollero

About the Author

CHRIS CEBOLLERO is an Internationally Recognized Leadership Specialist, Multi #1 Best Selling Author, Coach, and Motivational Lecturer. His dynamic and energetic speaking style has entertained, motivated, and educated individuals, groups, and teams for over 30 years. Chris is currently the President/CEO of his own consulting firm specializing in Leadership Development, Individual and Executive Coaching, and Organizational Process Improvement. Chris has been seen on ABC, NBC, CBS, and FOX. He is a Certified Member of the John Maxwell Team and is an Official Member of the Forbes Coaches Council. Chris has spent over 30 years in the Emergency Medical Services career field and continues to be an advocate for delivering the best care possible.

HIRE CHRIS FOR YOUR NEXT SPEAKING EVENT

Internationally Recognized Leadership Expert Chris Cebollero is available to speak at your live or virtual events. Chris creates custom presentations to meet your audiences' goals or goals of your event. Chris is available for:

- Keynote Addresses
- Facilitation
- Instructor Trainer Classes
- Workshops
- Lunch & Learn Sessions
- Single Day and Multi-week Mastermind Groups

Contact **julie@chriscebollero.com** and she will have all the details.

ULTIMATE COACHING

As an *Executive Director with the John Maxwell Team*, Chris can bring countless teachings from his friend and mentor John Maxwell to you and your organization. Topics Include:

- 21 Irrefutable Laws of Leadership
- 17 Indisputable Laws of Teamwork
- Good Leaders Ask Great Questions
- Developing the Leaders Around You
- Today Matters
- Leadership Gold
- Put Your Dreams to The Test
- 15 Invaluable Laws of Growth
- Becoming a Person of Influence
- How to Be a Real Success
- Everyone Communicates Few Connect

Contact **julie@chriscebollero.com** and she will have all the details.

Become a Fan of the Ultimate Leadership Podcast

Join Chris as he hosts the Ultimate Leadership Podcast. Chris brings in world experts in their fields of specialty to share their knowledge, insights, experience and to discuss the latest leadership, professional development and self-help topics.

www.ultimateleadership.blubrry.com

Other Leadership Books by Chris

Ultimate Leadership: 10 Rules for Success
Ultimate Success: Strategic Leadership Excellence
Dear Younger Self My Advice to You

You can find these books on Amazon or our home page of our website at www.chriscebollero.com

Bibliography

5 Reasons Why Feedback is Important, Retrieved from https://www.snapsurveys.com/blog/5-reasons-feedback-important/

WHY FEEDBACK IS IMPORTANT IN THE WORKPLACE, Retrieved from https://www.t-three.com/soak/insights/why-feedback-is-important

5 Reasons Why Feedback is Important, Retrieved from https://www.snapsurveys.com/blog/5-reasons-feedback-important/

4 Vital Elements of giving Constructive Feedback, Retrieved from https://collegeforadultlearning.edu.au/4-vital-elements-of-giving-constructive-feedback/

Four Key Elements for Offering Constructive Criticism Successfully, Retrieved from https://www.sandler.com/blog/four-key-elements-offering-constructive-criticism-successfully/

Why Giving Feedback At Work Doesn't Improve Performance, And What You Can Do About It, Retrieved from, https://www.forbes.com/sites/karlynborysenko/2019/03/19/why-giving-feedback-at-work-doesnt-improve-performance-and-what-you-can-do-about-it/#407691d329ba

Section 4. Providing Corrective Feedback, Retrieved from https://ctb.ku.edu/en/table-of contents/advocacy/encouragementeducation/corrective-feedback/main

Kinds of Feedback, Retrieved from, https://www.careerwave.me/coaching-tool/kinds-of-feedback/

9 Critical Components of Constructive Feedback, Retrieved from https://attorneyexecutivecoaching.com/9-critical-components-of-constructive-feedback/

People Management: Introduction to Motivation (GCSE) Retrieved from https://www.tutor2u.net/business/reference/people-management-introduction tomotivation#:~:text=A%20well%2Dmotivated%20workforce%20can,(amount%20produced%20per%20employee).&text=Lower%20levels%20of%20absenteeism%20as,of%20employees%20leaving%20the%20business).

7 Simple Ways to Lead by Example, Retrieved From https://www.inc.com/brent-gleeson/7-ways-to-lead-by-example.html

link of the Image that's attached above https://hr.williams.edu/files/2014/05/Coaching-Analysis_Handout.pdf

www.ingramcontent.com/pod-product-compliance
Lightning Source LLC
Chambersburg PA
CBHW070649220526
45466CB00001B/354